TRAIN

THE

BRAIN

TRAIN

THE

BRAIN

USE IT OR LOSE IT

Exercises, Tests and Puzzles
to Keep Your Brain
Super-fit!

Dr. Gareth Moore

JEREMY P. TARCHER

A MEMBER OF PENGUIN GROUP (USA) INC.

NEW YORK

JEREMY P. TARCHER/PENGUIN
Published by the Penguin Group
Penguin Group (USA) Inc., 375 Hudson Street, New York, New York
10014, USA • Penguin Group (Canada), 90 Eglinton Avenue East, Suite 700,
Toronto, Ontario M4P 2Y3, Canada (a division of Pearson Canada Inc.) •
Penguin Books Ltd, 80 Strand, London WC2R 0RL, England • Penguin Ireland,
25 St Stephen's Green, Dublin 2, Ireland (a division of Penguin Books Ltd) •
Penguin Group (Australia), 250 Camberwell Road, Camberwell,
Victoria 3124, Australia (a division of Pearson Australia Group Pty Ltd) •
Penguin Books India Pvt Ltd, 11 Community Centre, Panchsheel Park,
New Delhi–110 017, India • Penguin Group (NZ), 67 Apollo Drive, Rosedale,
North Shore 0632, New Zealand (a division of Pearson New Zealand Ltd) •
Penguin Books (South Africa) (Pty) Ltd, 24 Sturdee Avenue,
Rosebank, Johannesburg 2196, South Africa

Penguin Books Ltd, Registered Offices: 80 Strand, London WC2R 0RL, England

Most Tarcher/Penguin books are available at special quantity discounts for bulk
purchase for sales promotions, premiums, fund-raising, and educational needs. Special
books or book excerpts also can be created to fit specific needs. For details, write
Penguin Group (USA) Inc. Special Markets, 375 Hudson Street, New York, NY 10014.

Library of Congress Cataloging-in-Publication Data

Moore, Gareth, date.
Train the brain : use it or lose it : exercise, tests, and puzzles
to keep your brain super-fit! / Gareth Moore.
p.   cm.
ISBN 978-1-58542-753-6
1. Cognition—Problems, exercises, etc.   2. Intellect—Problems, exercises, etc.
3. Logic puzzles.   I. Title.
BF431.3.M68   2009   2009012756
153.4—dc22

Printed in the United States of America
1 3 5 7 9 10 8 6 4 2

Neither the publisher nor the author is engaged in rendering professional advice or services
to the individual reader. The ideas, procedures, and suggestions contained in this book are
not intended as a substitute for consulting with your physician. All matters regarding your
health require medical supervision. Neither the author nor the publisher shall be liable or
responsible for any loss or damage allegedly arising from any information or suggestion
in this book.

While the author has made every effort to provide accurate telephone numbers and
Internet addresses at the time of publication, neither the publisher nor the author assumes
any responsibility for errors, or for changes that occur after publication. Further, the publisher does not have any control over and does not assume any responsibility for author or
third-party websites or their content.

CONTENTS

Introduction

6

How to Use This Book

8

Beginner Exercises

9

Intermediate Exercises

69

Advanced Exercises

129

INTRODUCTION

Important brain functions such as memory, attention and processing speed can all be improved by training. If you want to remember more, concentrate better and think faster, start training your brain today—fight the mental flab and help ensure you use it rather than lose it!

Brain training is for everyone, from young adults through to the elderly. Continually challenging your brain encourages it to grow and develop—and, unlike a visit to a physical gym, entering the mind gym brings with it no risk of injury and no need for specialized equipment. Just yourself, this book and a pencil will start you off on the path to a mentally fitter you. So sharpen your pencil and sharpen your brain!

A number of factors affect your brain's efficiency. Food is one example. The brain has around one hundred billion neurons and each of these cells relies for its performance on the complex mix of minerals and vitamins we eat. It's probable that a diet high in mono- and polyunsaturated fats, found in both fish and olive oil, is good for our brains. Vitamin E, polyphenols and antioxidants may also help us avoid mental decline—citrus and dark-skinned fruits and vegetables are good choices.

Numerous studies have also shown that skipping breakfast is bad news for our brainpower throughout the day—and it's not ideal for the rest of the body either! A high-fiber breakfast that steadily releases glucose is good, such as beans on toast, for example. Sugary snacks and fizzy drinks for breakfast, however, have been shown to result in children's having poor memory and brief attention spans.

As well as a balanced diet, physical fitness is an important part of maintaining good mental well-being. Keeping the blood flowing is one of the best ways to help new brain cells grow, and cardiovascular health is important for preserving what you already have. You don't need to be super-fit—a sedate half-hour walk just three times a week can go a long way to improving your mental faculties, compared to a sedentary lifestyle.

Minimizing stress wherever possible is also a good way of avoiding mental decline. In fact, studies have shown that difficult decisions are often best solved by taking a break, and even by sleeping on them—our brains continue to process thoughts without us being actively conscious of the fact, and new ideas often occur to us when we are at our most relaxed. So sleep on that tough problem and you'll not only minimize the stress—you might solve it, too.

Some things aren't good for our brains—nicotine and alcohol, as well as other drugs, are bad for our mental health. Try to cut down on trans-fatty acids, found in cakes, pastries and biscuits, which may contribute to a range of mental problems. Our brains are sixty percent fat and trans-fats could clog them up.

A lack of sleep is definitely not good for you, either. If you have been awake for twenty-one hours straight then you are likely to have the degraded mental faculties of someone who is legally drunk. Successive late nights and early mornings can also have the same effect. Conversely, an extra hour or two in bed can help you concentrate and stay attentive—so an early night the day before an important interview or exam is a good plan.

What's particularly interesting is that studies suggest improvements from brain training don't just go away as soon as you finish the program. Research has shown that measurable gains can last not just months but many years, particularly for memory-training. A recent study of elderly people even revealed that brain training can result in memory performance equal to that of people over ten years younger.

With so much evidence in favor of brain training, you might wonder why we don't all do it every day. Perhaps you already do—something as simple as reading regularly has been shown to help. In fact, the real question in brain training is not whether your brain can be trained—there is plenty of scientific evidence that it can—but how best to go about doing it. That's why this book has been carefully designed to contain a wide range of tasks that exercise many different areas of your brain. And hopefully you'll have fun on the way to a sharper, smarter and faster you!

HOW TO USE THIS BOOK

This book is packed full of a variety of brain-training tasks. It is broken down into three sections and as you progress the tasks become somewhat trickier, so for maximum benefit it's best to start at the beginning and work your way through.

You should try to avoid skipping any of the puzzles or tasks, particularly if the reason is simply that you find them tricky—these are almost certainly the tasks that will be of most benefit to you. For example, if you find the memory challenges hard then this might mean you will have the most noticeable improvement from completing those tasks. If they really are too difficult then start by trying to remember just a few of the words and take it from there. Or, if you're truly stuck on a puzzle, turn the page and take a peek at the answer for a clue. It's meant to be fun and it shouldn't be too frustrating.

Most of the pages will probably only take you a few minutes to complete. Some might take you a little longer, and others will be quicker to do. Try to spend ten minutes or so each day on the tasks—perhaps two or three pages per day, depending on how hard you find the puzzles.

If you complete all the pages in the book you should be well on the way to a better mental you. For further challenges try some of the logical puzzles on my website, www.puzzlemix.com.

Good luck!

Which of these countries is the odd one out, and why?

France   Luxembourg   Denmark

Morocco   Greece   Croatia

Which number comes next in this sequence?

1   1   2   3   5   8   ____

On Tuesday I went to the bank, two days after I had
gone shopping, which was in turn six days after
my dental appointment. On which day of the week
did I see the dentist?

____

If it's 5:40p.m. in Britain then it is 12:40p.m. in New York since
New York is five hours behind. If it is the following times in
Britain, what time is it in New York?

7:50p.m.   6:20a.m.   3:15a.m.

____   ____   ____

If I roll a normal six-sided die, what is the likelihood that
I roll "3" twice in a row?

____

Look at the following list of animals and spend up to one minute
trying to memorize all eight words. Then turn the page and recall
as many as possible.

Giraffe   Elephant   Monkey   Goat
Squirrel   Camel   Llama   Dog

Which of these countries is the odd one out, and why?

Morocco, because all the other countries are on the continent of Europe.

Which number comes next in this sequence?

13 comes next. Each number is the sum of the preceding two numbers.

On Tuesday I went to the bank, two days after I had gone shopping, which was in turn six days after my dental appointment. On which day of the week did I see the dentist?

Monday.

If it's 5:40p.m. in Britain then it is 12:40p.m. in New York since New York is five hours behind. If it is the following times in Britain, what time is it in New York?

7:50p.m.   6:20a.m.   3:15a.m.

2:50p.m.   1:20a.m.   10:15p.m.

If I roll a normal six-sided die, what is the likelihood that I roll "3" twice in a row?

1 in 36, which is 1 in 6 times 1 in 6.

Recall the animals:

Can you place the numbers 1 to 9 into each of the empty boxes so that no number is used more than once and so that each of the arithmetic equations reading both across and down is correct?

You don't need to guess—only logic is required!

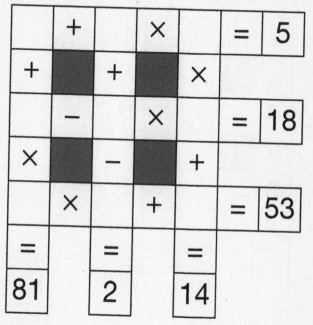

Work out values as if typing the sums into a calculator—so for example in the first column add the first two numbers before multiplying by the third.

The solution is:

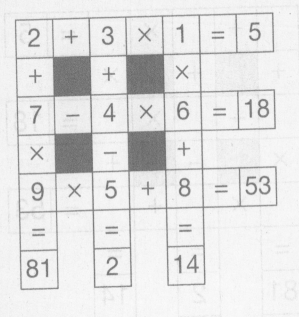

2	+	3	×	1	=	5
+		+		×		
7	−	4	×	6	=	18
×		−		+		
9	×	5	+	8	=	53
=		=		=		
81		2		14		

*Read the following colorful but prosaic story, and then answer as many questions as you can **without** referring back to the text. Once you have answered as many as you can, read the text straight through one more time and see if you can then answer the rest.*

James's favorite color was red, which matched the paint on the car filling his driveway. He was not a fan of his brother Simon's choice of a dark-green car—it looked too much like it was dressed in camouflage gear! Their sister Diane did not approve of any of the colors of the rainbow, much preferring white or black for her vehicles, which is perhaps why her pick-up truck was painted with alternating stripes of both. James thought it looked like a boiled sweet. Simon's friend Bob was a bright-colors person, specializing in vibrant oranges and yellows, particularly on the rather garish front door of his house.

What color is Simon's car?

What is the relationship between Bob and James?

What type of vehicle does Diane own?

Name two colors on Bob's front door.

What color is the car on James's driveway?

Which colors does Diane not approve of?

What color is Simon's car?

It is dark green.

What is the relationship between Bob and James?

Bob is James's brother's friend.

What type of vehicle does Diane own?

A pick-up truck.

Name two colors on Bob's front door.

Orange and yellow.

What color is the car on James's driveway?

Red.

Which colors does Diane not approve of?

Colors of the rainbow.

Look at this picture, then try to answer the following counting questions.

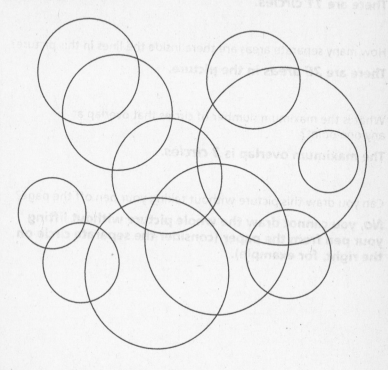

How many circles can you count in this picture? ____

How many separate areas are there inside the lines in this picture? ____

What is the maximum number of circles that overlap at any one point? ____

Can you draw this picture without taking your pen off the page? ____

How many circles can you count in this picture?

There are *11 circles*.

How many separate areas are there inside the lines in this picture?

There are *26 areas* in the picture.

What is the maximum number of circles that overlap at any one point?

The maximum overlap is *3 circles*.

Can you draw this picture without taking your pen off the page?

***No*, you cannot draw the whole picture without lifting your pen from the paper (consider the separate circle on the right, for example).**

Look at the following picture. In just one minute see if you can reproduce it precisely as if reflected in the horizontal line "mirror." Draw the result on the empty grid below the mirror line.

The reflected picture should look like this:

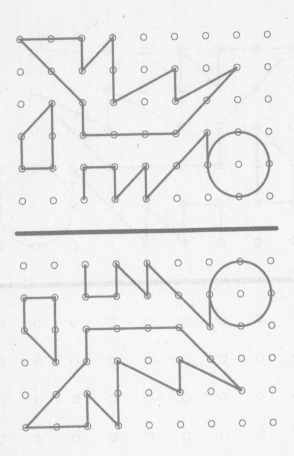

Can you find a 9-square-long path in this number maze that moves from square to square by applying the operation "+4"? Squares must touch horizontally or vertically.

For example, the 20 at the top-left could connect to the 24 directly below, because applying "+4" to 20 gives 24.

20	16	6	10	14
24	4	8	16	12
22	20	12	16	18
12	36	26	20	22
46	32	28	24	12

Now try to find a second path of 13 squares by applying "+2," but this time you may also move to diagonally touching squares.

The solutions are:

Look at the following list of colors for up to two minutes. On the following page you will find the same list of words but in a different order—turn the page and see how accurately you can recall the correct positioning of the words.

Green	Orange	Purple
Cyan	Indigo	Scarlet
White	Brown	Silver

MISSING WORDS 1

Once you have completed and checked the above task, try this one. Look at these two lists of words, then turn the page and try to spot which word is missing from each list.

Liberal	Democrat	Green
	Socialist	Conservative

Eleanor	Sheba	Victoria
	Helen	Elizabeth

Try to place the words back in the appropriate boxes:

	Purple	Orange	Green
	Indigo	Scarlet	Cyan
	Silver		White

Brown	Indigo	Scarlet
Cyan	Orange	Silver
Green	Purple	White

MISSING WORDS 1

Can you spot which word is missing from each list?

Conservative   **Liberal**   _____

   Green   **Democrat**

Victoria   **Elizabeth**   _____

   Sheba   **Eleanor**

Try to complete the following arithmetic problems as quickly as possible:

18 − 15 = ☐   11 + 64 = ☐

69 − 2 = ☐   92 − 7 = ☐

8 + 3 = ☐   9 × 10 = ☐

60 + 19 = ☐   14 + 94 = ☐

4 + 64 = ☐   17 + 2 = ☐

10 × 10 = ☐   9 × 7 = ☐

2 × 5 = ☐   6 × 8 = ☐

77 − 8 = ☐   72 − 12 = ☐

☐ − 8 = 74   ☐ − 1 = 71

32 + ☐ = 46   ☐ × 5 = 50

☐ − 5 = 17   ☐ + 54 = 57

☐ − 4 = 44   17 + ☐ = 88

4 + ☐ = 17   59 − ☐ = 50

☐ + 7 = 78   48 + ☐ = 59

The solutions are:

$18 - 15 =$	**3**	$11 + 64 =$	**75**
$69 - 2 =$	**67**	$92 - 7 =$	**85**
$8 + 3 =$	**11**	$9 \times 10 =$	**90**
$60 + 19 =$	**79**	$14 + 94 =$	**108**
$4 + 64 =$	**68**	$17 + 2 =$	**19**
$10 \times 10 =$	**100**	$9 \times 7 =$	**63**
$2 \times 5 =$	**10**	$6 \times 8 =$	**48**
$77 - 8 =$	**69**	$72 - 12 =$	**60**

$\boxed{82} - 8 = 74$ $\qquad$ $\boxed{72} - 1 = 71$

$32 + \boxed{14} = 46$ $\qquad$ $\boxed{10} \times 5 = 50$

$\boxed{22} - 5 = 17$ $\qquad$ $\boxed{3} + 54 = 57$

$\boxed{48} - 4 = 44$ $\qquad$ $17 + \boxed{71} = 88$

$4 + \boxed{13} = 17$ $\qquad$ $59 - \boxed{9} = 50$

$\boxed{71} + 7 = 78$ $\qquad$ $48 + \boxed{11} = 59$

Can you work out which three of the shapes at the bottom of this page can be joined together to make this pyramid shape? None of the pieces can be rotated or turned over.

The three shapes that make up the pyramid are shaded below, and the two possible ways of arranging them to form the pyramid are shown:

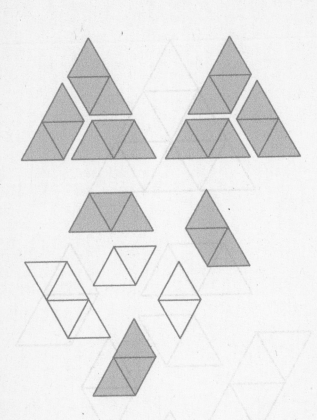

Fill in the empty bricks in this number pyramid. Each brick must contain a number equal to the sum of the two bricks directly below it.

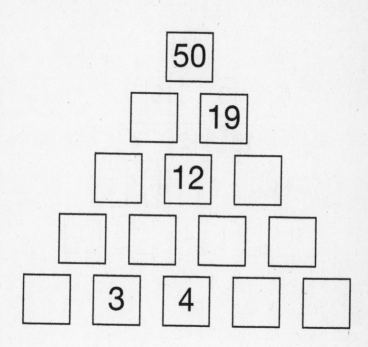

The solution is:

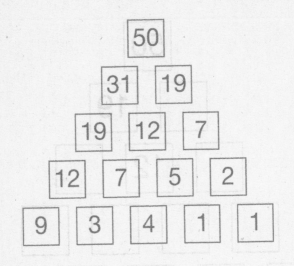

Can you draw three straight lines in order to divide this shape into four separate areas? The lines may touch but they must not cross. Each area must contain precisely one star, one circle and one hexagon.

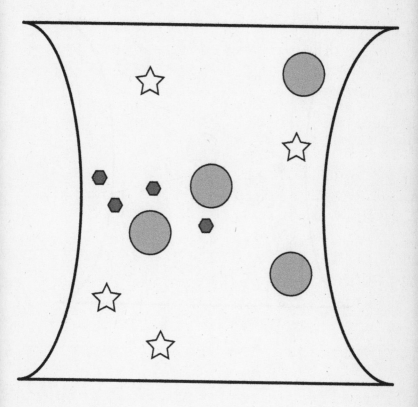

The solution is:

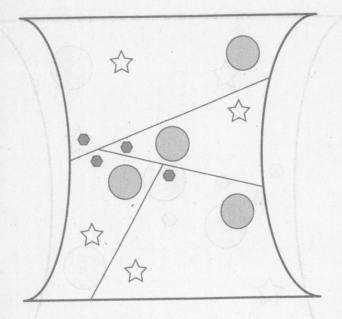

See if you can work out how much time has elapsed between each of these pairs of times.

6:45a.m. to 12:05p.m. = [:]

2:40p.m. to   6:00p.m. = [:]

5:40a.m. to   9:25a.m. = [:]

2:55p.m. to 11:00p.m. = [:]

3:30a.m. to   5:55p.m. = [:]

2:15a.m. to   6:30p.m. = [:]

7:50a.m. to 12:45p.m. = [:]

4:05a.m. to 11:15a.m. = [:]

10:45a.m. to   8:30p.m. = [:]

2:00a.m. to   7:00p.m. = [:]

9:30p.m. to   9:45p.m. = [:]

3:15a.m. to   2:40p.m. = [:]

6:45a.m. to   9:35a.m. = [:]

12:50p.m. to   5:05p.m. = [:]

The solutions are:

6:45a.m. to 12:05p.m. = **5:20**

2:40p.m. to 6:00p.m. = **3:20**

5:40a.m. to 9:25a.m. = **3:45**

2:55p.m. to 11:00p.m. = **8:05**

3:30a.m. to 5:55p.m. = **14:25**

2:15a.m. to 6:30p.m. = **16:15**

7:50a.m. to 12:45p.m. = **4:55**

4:05a.m. to 11:15a.m. = **7:10**

10:45a.m. to 8:30p.m. = **9:45**

2:00a.m. to 7:00p.m. = **17:00**

9:30p.m. to 9:45p.m. = **0:15**

3:15a.m. to 2:40p.m. = **11:25**

6:45a.m. to 9:35a.m. = **2:50**

12:50p.m. to 5:05p.m. = **4:15**

Which of these sports is the odd one out, and why?

Croquet	Darts	Golf
Tennis	Billiards	Shooting

Which number comes next in this sequence?

15	22	30	39	49

If I toss a coin twice, what is the likelihood that I get heads up both times?

I was 24 years old by the time 1972 began, so how old was I when 1995 ended?

On Tuesday I drive to work at an average of 30m.p.h. (miles per hour) and get there in 20 minutes. How far away is my work?

If I fly from Sydney to Los Angeles on an eight-hour flight and arrive at 3:30p.m., what time did I leave Sydney given that Sydney is nine hours ahead of London while Los Angeles is eight hours behind?

Look at the following list of words and spend up to one minute trying to memorize all eight words. Then turn the page and recall as many as possible.

Cabin	Hotel	Hut	House
Igloo	Lodge	Inn	Chalet

Which of these sports is the odd one out, and why?

***Tennis*, because all the other sports require you to aim at specific targets.**

Which number comes next in this sequence?

60 comes next. The difference between successive numbers increases by 1 at each step.

If I toss a coin twice, what is the likelihood that I get heads up both times?

1 in 4.

I was 24 years old by the time 1972 began, so how old was I when 1995 ended?

48 years old.

On Tuesday I drive to work at an average of 30m.p.h. (miles per hour) and get there in 20 minutes. How far away is my work?

10 miles away.

If I fly from Sydney to Los Angeles on an eight-hour flight and arrive at 3:30p.m., what time did I leave Sydney given that Sydney is nine hours ahead of London while Los Angeles is eight hours behind?

***12:30a.m.* 3:30p.m. LA is 11:30p.m. London, or 8:30a.m. Sydney. So I left at 12:30a.m.**

Recall the buildings:

Look at the following picture for up to two minutes, then rotate the book *anticlockwise* and cover over the top half of the page. Now try to reproduce the picture on the empty grid.

Now rotate the book back, uncover the top half again and check for and correct any mistakes.

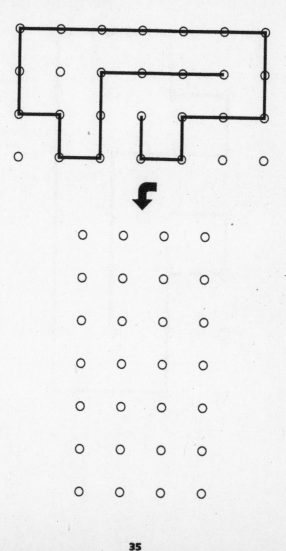

The rotated version of the picture should look like this:

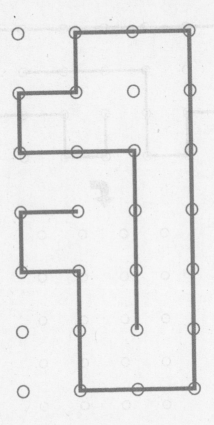

Look at this picture, then try to answer the following counting questions.

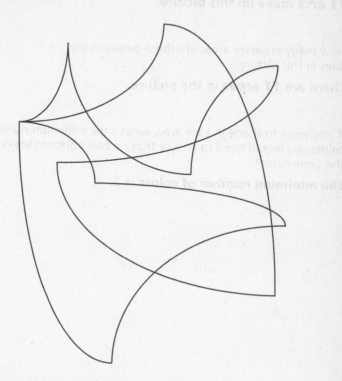

How many arcs—individual curves—can you count in this picture?

_____

How many separate areas are there between the lines in this picture?

_____

If you were to shade in each area, what's the minimum number of colors you would need to ensure that no two adjacent areas were the same color?

_____

How many arcs—individual curves—can you count in this picture?

11 *arcs* make up this picture.

How many separate areas are there between the
lines in this picture?

There are 11 *areas* in the picture.

If you were to shade in each area, what's the minimum number of
colors you would need to ensure that no two adjacent areas were
the same color?

The minimum number of colors is 2.

Can you place the numbers 1 to 9 into each of the empty boxes so that no number is used more than once and so that each of the arithmetic equations reading both across and down is correct?

You don't need to guess—only logic is required!

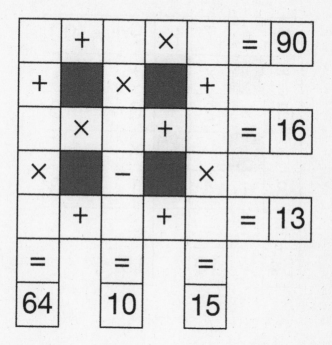

Work out values as if typing the sums into a calculator—so, for example, in the first column add the first two numbers before multiplying by the third.

The solution is:

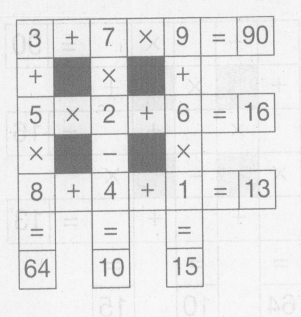

If you were to cut out this shape net consisting of four adjacent triangles and fold it up into a pyramid, which of the four pictures below would be visible by rotating the pyramid appropriately?

a

b

c

d

The only arrangement that would be visible is:

d

Look at these numbers:

13   16   37   4
       23   8   24

Can you find two numbers which add together to make a third?

____ + ____ = ____

Now find a different set of two numbers which add together to
make a third number.

____ + ____ = ____

How many of these numbers result in a whole number
when divided by 4?   ____

And how many of these are prime numbers
(only divisible by themselves and one)?   ____

Can you find two numbers which add together to make a third? And a different set?

The two sets are:

$$13 + 24 = 37$$

$$8 + 16 = 24$$

How many of these numbers result in a whole number when divided by 4?

4 result in a whole number. These are 4, 8, 16 and 24.

And how many are prime numbers (only divisible by themselves and one)?

3 prime numbers, which are 13, 23 and 37.

*Read the following healthy eating story, and then answer as many questions as you can **without** referring back to the text. Once you have answered as many as you can, read the text straight through one more time and see if you can then answer the rest.*

It's important to be fruity. Five a day is the maxim, although it varies from country to country. The World Health Organization estimates 1 in 10 cancers is due to lack of fruit and vegetables, and 2.7 million lives a year could be saved!

At least 400 grams a day of non-starchy fruit and vegetables can not only protect from cancer, but could prevent over ten percent of strokes. They probably protect against obesity and reduce the risk of diabetes. There are many hundreds of different fruits grown for human consumption.

How many lives a year could be saved by eating more fruit and vegetables?

What fruity maxim is given at the start?

What is the minimum recommended weight of fruit and vegetables to consume each day?

What percentage of strokes could be avoided?

And how many cancers might never happen?

Name two other things protected against?

How many times is the word "fruit" or its plural or adjectival forms used?

How many lives a year could be saved by eating more fruit and vegetables?

2.7 million.

What fruity maxim is given at the start?

"Five a day."

What is the minimum recommended weight of fruit and vegetables to consume each day?

400 grams.

What percentage of strokes could be avoided?

Over 10%.

And how many cancers might never happen?

1 in 10.

Name two other things protected against?

Obesity and diabetes.

How many times is the word "fruit" or its plural or adjectival forms used?

4 times, including the adjective "fruity."

Fill in the empty bricks in this number pyramid. Each brick must contain a number equal to the sum of the two bricks directly below it.

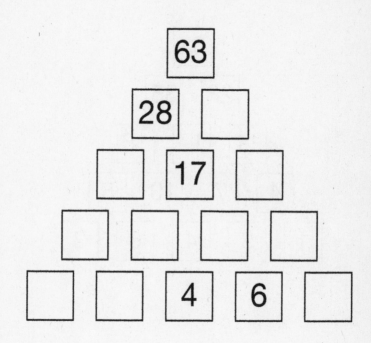

The solution is:

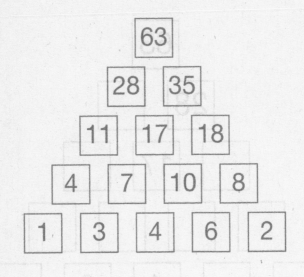

See if you can work out how much time has elapsed between each of these pairs of times.

3:05a.m. to 10:35a.m. = [:]

1:55a.m. to 2:05p.m. = [:]

3:50a.m. to 11:25p.m. = [:]

12:30a.m. to 3:20p.m. = [:]

2:05a.m. to 6:30a.m. = [:]

10:50a.m. to 8:45p.m. = [:]

8:05p.m. to 10:45p.m. = [:]

11:45a.m. to 4:35p.m. = [:]

12:10p.m. to 10:55p.m. = [:]

9:00a.m. to 10:25a.m. = [:]

7:05a.m. to 9:00a.m. = [:]

12:15a.m. to 3:35a.m. = [:]

4:05p.m. to 6:20p.m. = [:]

4:05a.m. to 4:05p.m. = [:]

The solutions are:

3:05a.m. to 10:35a.m. = **7:30**

1:55a.m. to 2:05p.m. = **12:10**

3:50a.m. to 11:25p.m. = **19:35**

12:30a.m. to 3:20p.m. = **14:50**

2:05a.m. to 6:30a.m. = **4:25**

10:50a.m. to 8:45p.m. = **9:55**

8:05p.m. to 10:45p.m. = **2:40**

11:45a.m. to 4:35p.m. = **4:50**

12:10p.m. to 10:55p.m. = **10:45**

9:00a.m. to 10:25a.m. = **1:25**

7:05a.m. to 9:00a.m. = **1:55**

12:15a.m. to 3:35a.m. = **3:20**

4:05p.m. to 6:20p.m. = **2:15**

4:05a.m. to 4:05p.m. = **12:00**

Look at the following picture. In just one minute see if you can reproduce it precisely as if reflected in the horizontal line "mirror." Draw the result on the empty grid below the mirror line.

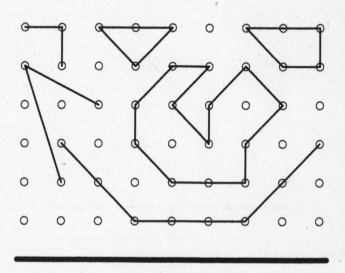

The reflected picture should look like this:

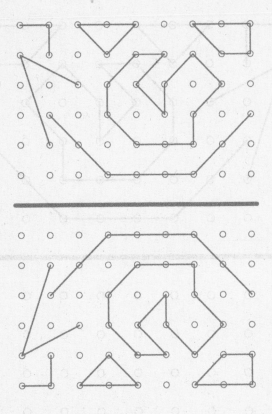

Look at the following list of games for up to two minutes. On the following page you will find the same list of words but in a different order—turn the page and see how accurately you can recall the correct positioning of the words.

Ludo	Bingo	Checkers
Go	Chess	Drafts
Mastermind	Marbles	Mah-jong

MISSING WORDS 2

Once you have completed the above task, try this one. Look at these two lists of words, then turn the page and try to spot which word is missing from each list.

Tunisia　　　　　　Morocco　　　　　Ethiopia

　　　Kenya　　　　　　　Egypt

Tennis　　　　Ping-pong　　　　　Squash

　　Racquetball　　　　Badminton

Try to place the words back in the appropriate boxes:

	Checkers	Bingo
	Draffs	Chess
Mastermind	Marbles	Mah-jong

Bingo	Drafts	Mah-jong
Chess	Go	Marbles
Checkers	Ludo	Mastermind

MISSING WORDS 2

Can you spot which word is missing from each list?

Egypt   **Tunisia**   _____

          Ethiopia   **Morocco**

Ping-pong   **Badminton**   _____

          Tennis   **Squash**

Can you find a 12-square-long path in this number maze that moves from square to square by applying the operation "−3"? Squares must touch horizontally or vertically.

For example, the 37 at the bottom-right could connect to the 34 directly to its left, because applying "−3" to 37 gives 34.

37	49	55	61	37
43	31	46	43	67
25	16	13	40	43
22	19	22	37	40
25	28	31	34	37

Now try to find a second path of 10 squares by applying "−6," but this time you may also move to diagonally touching squares.

The solutions are:

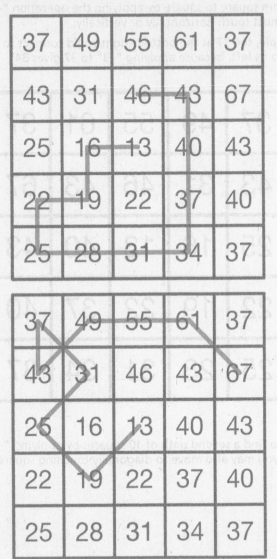

If you were to cut out this shape net consisting of four adjacent triangles and fold it up into a pyramid, which of the four pictures below would be visible by rotating the pyramid appropriately?

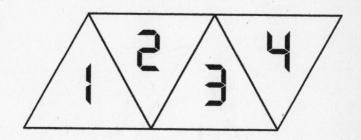

a

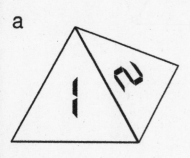

b

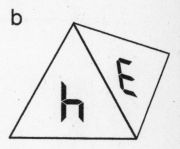

c

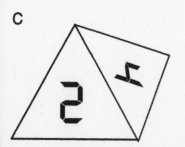

d

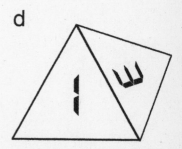

The only arrangement that would be visible is:

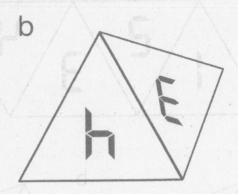

Try to complete the following arithmetic problems as quickly as possible:

$29 - 18 =$ [   ]

$37 - 4 =$ [   ]

$65 - 13 =$ [   ]

$81 - 6 =$ [   ]

$7 \times 11 =$ [   ]

$25 - 10 =$ [   ]

$55 - 9 =$ [   ]

$107 - 13 =$ [   ]

$7 \times 3 =$ [   ]

$82 - 8 =$ [   ]

$37 - 19 =$ [   ]

$4 + 7 =$ [   ]

$4 \times 12 =$ [   ]

$37 - 18 =$ [   ]

$69 - 4 =$ [   ]

$94 - 12 =$ [   ]

[   ] $+ 20 = 30$

$16 +$ [   ] $= 61$

$87 +$ [   ] $= 107$

$25 -$ [   ] $= 17$

$59 -$ [   ] $= 46$

[   ] $- 6 = 91$

[   ] $- 16 = 82$

$8 \times$ [   ] $= 64$

[   ] $- 9 = 47$

[   ] $+ 3 = 29$

$9 +$ [   ] $= 107$

[   ] $- 4 = 86$

The solutions are:

$29 - 18 =$ **11** $\qquad$ $37 - 4 =$ **33**

$65 - 13 =$ **52** $\qquad$ $81 - 6 =$ **75**

$7 \times 11 =$ **77** $\qquad$ $25 - 10 =$ **15**

$55 - 9 =$ **46** $\qquad$ $107 - 13 =$ **94**

$7 \times 3 =$ **21** $\qquad$ $82 - 8 =$ **74**

$37 - 19 =$ **18** $\qquad$ $4 + 7 =$ **11**

$4 \times 12 =$ **48** $\qquad$ $37 - 18 =$ **19**

$69 - 4 =$ **65** $\qquad$ $94 - 12 =$ **82**

10 $+ 20 = 30$ $\qquad$ $16 +$ **45** $= 61$

$87 +$ **20** $= 107$ $\qquad$ $25 -$ **8** $= 17$

$59 -$ **13** $= 46$ $\qquad$ **97** $- 6 = 91$

98 $- 16 = 82$ $\qquad$ $8 \times$ **8** $= 64$

56 $- 9 = 47$ $\qquad$ **26** $+ 3 = 29$

$9 +$ **98** $= 107$ $\qquad$ **90** $- 4 = 86$

Can you work out which four of the shapes at the bottom of this page can be joined together to make this square shape? None of the pieces can be rotated or turned over.

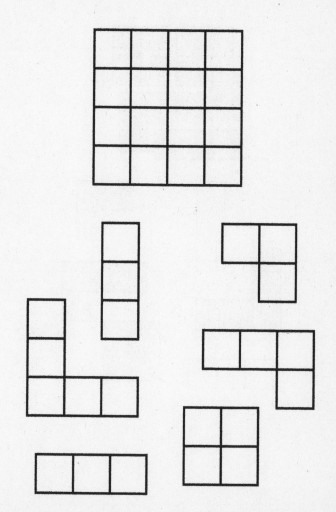

The four shapes that make up the square are shaded below, and their arrangement to form the square is shown:

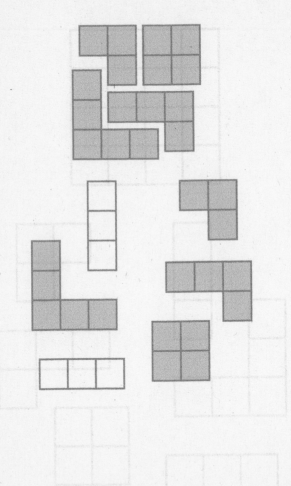

Look at the following picture for up to two minutes, then rotate the book *clockwise* and cover over the top half of the page. Now try to reproduce the picture on the empty grid.

Now rotate the book back, uncover the top half again and check for and correct any mistakes.

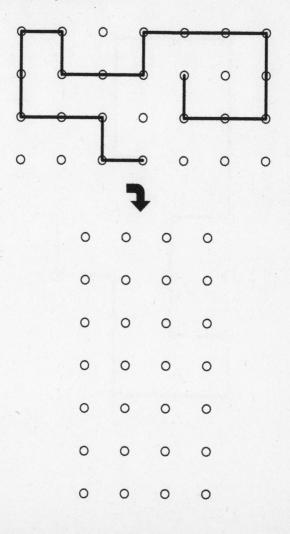

The rotated version of the picture should look like this:

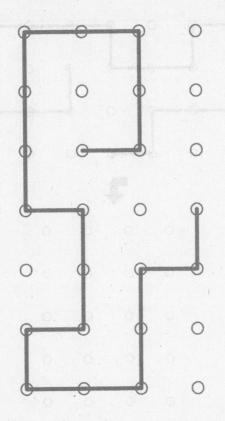

Consider these numbers:

25   17   9   11

      14   6   4

Can you find two numbers which add together to make a third?

___ + ___ = ___

Now find a different set of two numbers which add together to make a third number.

___ + ___ = ___

What is the result of adding together all 7 numbers?   ___

Can any pair of these numbers be divided one into the other in order to result in a whole number?   ___

Can you find two numbers which add together to make a third?
And a different set?

The two sets are:

$$6 + 11 = 17$$

$$11 + 14 = 25$$

What is the result of adding together all 7 numbers?

86.

Can any pair of these numbers be divided one into the other in
order to result in a whole number?

No. **All pairs result in fractional numbers.**

Can you draw three straight lines in order to divide this shape into four separate areas? The lines may touch but they must not cross. Each area must contain precisely one star, one circle and one hexagon.

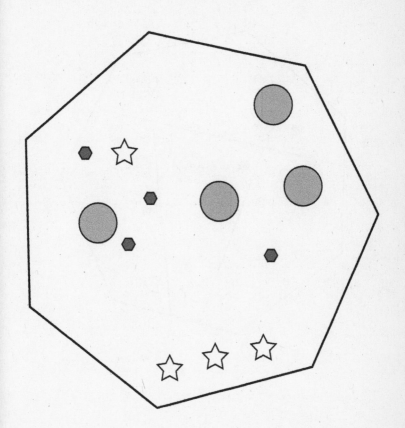

The solution is:

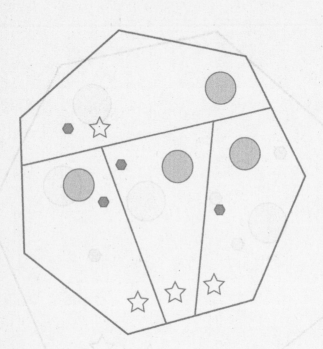

Can you place the numbers 1 to 9 into each of the empty boxes so that no number is used more than once and so that each of the arithmetic equations reading both across and down is correct?

You don't need to guess—only logic is required!

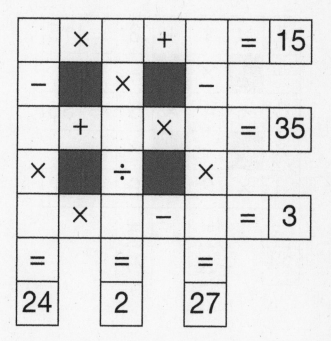

Work out values as if typing the sums into a calculator—so for example in the middle row add the first two numbers before multiplying by the third.

The solution is:

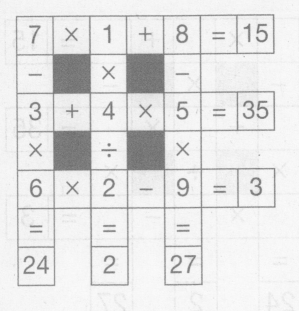

7	×	1	+	8	=	15
−		×		−		
3	+	4	×	5	=	35
×		÷		×		
6	×	2	−	9	=	3
=		=		=		
24		2		27		

Can you draw three straight lines in order to divide this shape into four separate areas? The lines may touch but they must not cross. Each area must contain precisely one star, one circle and one hexagon.

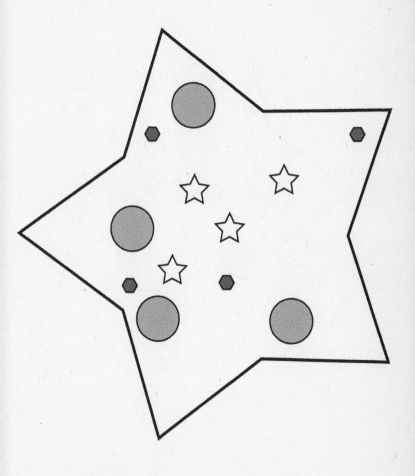

The solution is:

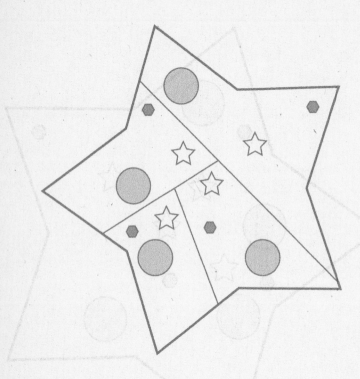

Which of these words is the odd one out, and why?

Scalene	Acute	Obtuse
Right	Wrong	Convex

Which number comes next in this sequence?

3	6	12	24	48	_____

If I take one card at random from a deck of 2 red and
2 black cards, then take a second card, what is the
likelihood I get two red cards?   _____

Ruth has 15 apples, but gives two-thirds to Simon.
He then eats half of what he has before giving 40% of the
remainder to me. How many apples do I now have?   _____

A 1-mile-long train enters a tunnel at 60 miles per hour.
If the tunnel is 5 miles in length, for how long is any part
of the train in the tunnel?   _____

How many even numbers are there between 1 and 99?   _____

Look at the following list of deserts and spend up to one minute
trying to memorize all eight words. Then turn the page and recall
as many as possible.

Gobi	Kalahari	Sahara	Mojave
Thar	Arabian	Great-Sandy	Atacama

Which of these words is the odd one out, and why?

Wrong—the rest are types of angle in geometry.

Which number comes next in this sequence?

96—the number doubles at each step.

If I take one card at random from a deck of 2 red and 2 black cards, then take a second card, what is the likelihood I get two red cards?

1 in 6, or 2 in 12. That is, 2 in 4 times 1 in 3.

Ruth has 15 apples, but gives two-thirds to Simon. He then eats half of what he has before giving 40% of the remainder to me. How many apples do I now have?

2 apples. Simon has 10, eats 5 and gives 2 to me.

A 1-mile-long train enters a tunnel at 60 miles per hour. If the tunnel is 5 miles in length, for how long is any part of the train in the tunnel?

6 minutes. The train is 1 mile long so it must travel the length of the tunnel plus one extra mile along the track while some part of the train is still inside the tunnel. That is, 5 + 1 miles.

How many even numbers are there between 1 and 99?

49. (2, 4, 6 . . . 96, 98).

Recall the deserts:

Look at the following list of shapes for up to two minutes. On the following page you will find the same list of words but in a different order—turn the page and see how accurately you can recall the correct positioning of the words.

Triangle	Diamond	Kite	Square
Pentagon	Hexagon	Rhombus	Trapezium
Circle	Rectangle	Ellipse	Octagon

MISSING WORDS 3

Once you have completed the above task, try this one. Look at these two lists of words, then turn the page and try to spot which word is missing from each list.

Sheep	Cow	Pig
Goat	Chicken	Bull

Future	Past	Immediately
Yesterday	Now	Never

Try to place the words back in the appropriate boxes:

Circle	Kite	Rhombus
Diamond	Octagon	Square
Ellipse	Pentagon	Triangle
Hexagon	Rectangle	Trapezium

MISSING WORDS 3

Can you spot which word is missing from each list?

Pig	Chicken	Bull
Cow	Sheep	_____

Immediately	Now	Never
Future	Yesterday	_____

What is the longest path you can find in this number maze that moves from square to square by applying the operation "+13"? Squares must touch horizontally or vertically. Mark it in.

For example, the 103 on the bottom row could connect to the 116 directly to its right, because applying "+13" to 103 gives 116.

84	75	66	57	39
53	65	3	30	48
42	29	16	12	21
55	95	107	120	133
68	81	94	103	116

Now try to find a second path by applying "+9," but this time you may also move to diagonally touching squares. Mark in the longest path you can find.

The solutions are:

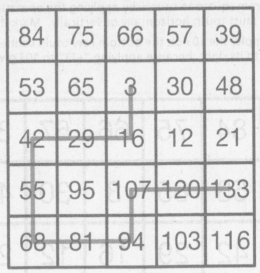

84	75	66	57	39
53	65	3	30	48
42	29	16	12	21
55	95	107	120	133
68	81	94	103	116

11 squares

84	75	66	57	39
53	65	3	30	48
42	29	16	12	21
55	95	107	120	133
68	81	94	103	116

10 squares

*Read the following tale of tails, and then answer as many questions as you can **without** referring back to the text. Once you have answered as many as you can, read the text straight through one more time and see if you can then answer the rest.*

In another world, I might be a hamster. It might be a gn-awful thought, but I can put a positive spin on it. Hamsters are good at spinning, at least in wheels. Or is that gerbils? I'm not really sure. It's all in the tail I think.

As a hamster, I'd change the law. More hamster rights: bigger cages, better food, less prodding. Not that I've ever owned a hamster, but I'm sure this makes sense. And there's another one—legal emancipation for hamsters. Hamsters want to run away, live a gn-awesome life and be generally g-naughty.

What four rights would hamsters gain if my hamster self changed the law?

What are hamsters said to be good at?

How many g- or gn- puns were there?

And what were these g- or gn- words?

What hamster-gerbil difference is stated?

What three general hamster desires are given at the end of the tale?

How many times is the word "hamster" or "hamsters" used?

What four rights would hamsters gain if my hamster self changed the law?

Bigger cages; better food; less prodding; legal emancipation.

What are hamsters said to be good at?

Spinning.

How many g- or gn- puns were there?

Three.

And what were these g- or gn- words?

Gn-awful; gn-awesome; g-naughty.

What hamster-gerbil difference is stated?

The tail.

What three general hamster desires are given at the end of the tale?

To run away; to live a gn-awesome life; to be generally g-naughty.

How many times is the word "hamster" or "hamsters" used?

7 times.

Look at the following picture. In just one minute see if you can reproduce it precisely as if reflected in the vertical line "mirror." Draw the result on the empty grid to the right of the mirror line.

The reflected picture should look like this:

See if you can work out how much time has elapsed between each of these pairs of times.

6:10a.m. to 7:05p.m. = [:]

2:10a.m. to 2:20a.m. = [:]

5:30a.m. to 7:45a.m. = [:]

12:45a.m. to 4:30a.m. = [:]

5:55a.m. to 3:00p.m. = [:]

9:50a.m. to 1:05p.m. = [:]

10:15a.m. to 5:30p.m. = [:]

10:15a.m. to 11:35p.m. = [:]

12:10a.m. to 6:20a.m. = [:]

12:40a.m. to 9:05a.m. = [:]

3:30p.m. to 10:10p.m. = [:]

5:10a.m. to 7:25p.m. = [:]

1:05a.m. to 12:55p.m. = [:]

10:40a.m. to 11:50p.m. = [:]

The solutions are:

6:10a.m.	to	7:05p.m. =	**12:55**
2:10a.m.	to	2:20a.m. =	**0:10**
5:30a.m.	to	7:45a.m. =	**2:15**
12:45a.m.	to	4:30a.m. =	**3:45**
5:55a.m.	to	3:00p.m. =	**9:05**
9:50a.m.	to	1:05p.m. =	**3:15**
10:15a.m.	to	5:30p.m. =	**7:15**
10:15a.m.	to	11:35p.m. =	**13:20**
12:10a.m.	to	6:20a.m. =	**6:10**
12:40a.m.	to	9:05a.m. =	**8:25**
3:30p.m.	to	10:10p.m. =	**6:40**
5:10a.m.	to	7:25p.m. =	**14:15**
1:05a.m.	to	12:55p.m. =	**11:50**
10:40a.m.	to	11:50p.m. =	**13:10**

Fill in the empty bricks in this number pyramid. Each brick must contain a number equal to the sum of the two bricks directly below it.

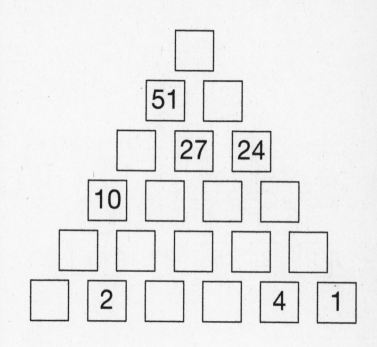

The solution is:

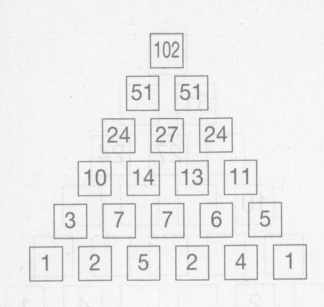

Look at this picture, then try to answer the following counting
questions.

How many triangles can you find in this picture? ____

And how many rectangles can you count? ____

How many triangles can you find in this picture?

There are *29 triangles* in this picture.

And how many rectangles can you count?

***9 rectangles* can be counted.**

Consider these numbers:

12   **7**   **25**   **16**

     14   **18**   **26**

Can you find two numbers which add together to make a third?

____ + ____ = ____

Now find a different set of two numbers which add together to make a third number.

____ + ____ = ____

What is the median of these numbers? In other words,
which is the middle number when sorted by value?   ____

Find two sets of three numbers that sum to 44:

____ + ____ + ____ = 44

____ + ____ + ____ = 44

Can you find two numbers which add together to make a third? And a different set?

The two sets are:

$$18 + 7 = 25$$
$$12 + 14 = 26$$

What is the median of these numbers? In other words, which is the middle number when sorted by value?

16.

Find two sets of three numbers that sum to 44:

$$7 + 12 + 25 = 44$$
$$12 + 14 + 18 = 44$$

Can you work out which of the shapes at the bottom of this page can be joined together to make the larger shape at the top? None of the pieces can be rotated or turned over, and no shape can be used more than once.

The solution and shapes are:

Look at the following picture for up to two minutes, then rotate the book *anticlockwise* and cover over the top half of the page. Now try to reproduce the picture on the empty grid.

Now rotate the book back, uncover the top half again and check for and correct any mistakes.

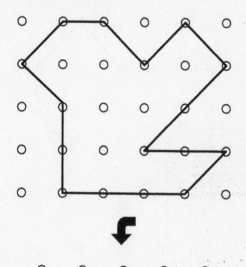

The rotated version of the picture should look like this:

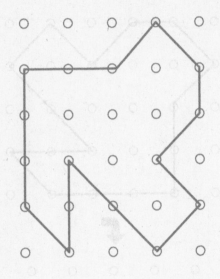

Try to complete the following arithmetic problems as quickly as possible:

2 × 8 =

66 + 15 =

48 + 10 =

88 − 1 =

69 − 14 =

11 + 56 =

12 × 10 =

6 + 87 =

1 + 90 =

6 × 7 =

70 + 5 =

72 + 5 =

59 − 1 =

59 + 15 =

12 + 20 =

17 − 8 =

× 4 = 36

× 2 = 24

− 2 = 81

94 + = 110

× 10 = 70

3 × = 27

+ 47 = 53

2 × = 18

× 8 = 32

× 6 = 30

+ 18 = 38

+ 8 = 49

The solutions are:

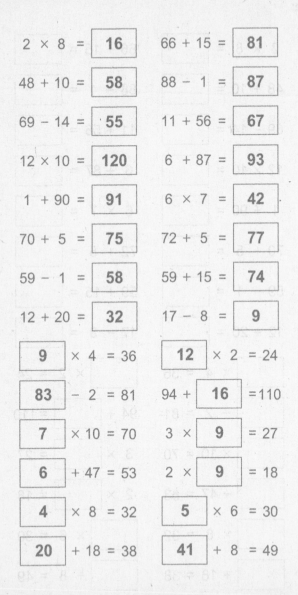

$2 \times 8 = \boxed{16}$ $66 + 15 = \boxed{81}$

$48 + 10 = \boxed{58}$ $88 - 1 = \boxed{87}$

$69 - 14 = \boxed{55}$ $11 + 56 = \boxed{67}$

$12 \times 10 = \boxed{120}$ $6 + 87 = \boxed{93}$

$1 + 90 = \boxed{91}$ $6 \times 7 = \boxed{42}$

$70 + 5 = \boxed{75}$ $72 + 5 = \boxed{77}$

$59 - 1 = \boxed{58}$ $59 + 15 = \boxed{74}$

$12 + 20 = \boxed{32}$ $17 - 8 = \boxed{9}$

$\boxed{9} \times 4 = 36$ $\boxed{12} \times 2 = 24$

$\boxed{83} - 2 = 81$ $94 + \boxed{16} = 110$

$\boxed{7} \times 10 = 70$ $3 \times \boxed{9} = 27$

$\boxed{6} + 47 = 53$ $2 \times \boxed{9} = 18$

$\boxed{4} \times 8 = 32$ $\boxed{5} \times 6 = 30$

$\boxed{20} + 18 = 38$ $\boxed{41} + 8 = 49$

Fill in the empty bricks in this number pyramid. Each brick must contain a number equal to the sum of the two bricks directly below it.

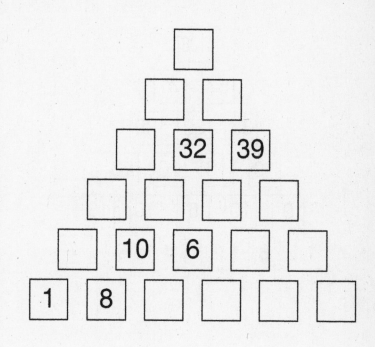

The solution is:

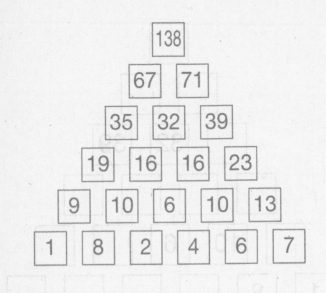

If you were to cut out this shape net consisting of four adjacent triangles and fold it up into a pyramid, which of the four pictures below would be visible by rotating the pyramid appropriately?

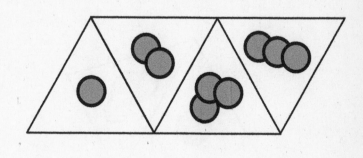

a

b

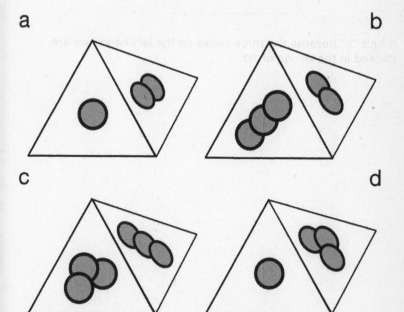

c

d

The only arrangement that would be visible is:

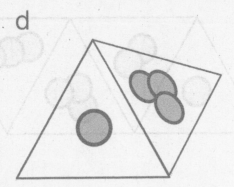

It isn't "c" because the three circles on the left-hand face are stacked in the wrong order.

*Read the following florid flutterings, and then answer as many questions as you can **without** referring back to the text. Once you have answered as many as you can, read the text straight through one more time and see if you can then answer the rest.*

Down at the flower shop, Rose's favorite flowers are gerberas while Hyacinth's are roses. Not just any roses, mind you, but big and tall ones with a bright color; in particular yellow or orange. Rose's fascination with daisy-like blooms extends to Japanese anemones—particularly the purple ones.

Were they to choose their namesake flowers, Rose would go for Maiden's Blush because of the scent. Hyacinth, meanwhile, would pick Ostara because of the violet-blue hue. Picking their joint favorite wasn't easy, but they settled on gladioli—in particular on the modern Stromboli with its large red flowers in mid-summer.

What is the favorite flower of Rose?

What other daisy-like bloom is she fond of?

Can you name two colors of her favorite flower that Hyacinth particularly likes?

What variety of rose would Rose pick?

What color of her namesake flower would Hyacinth choose?

For their joint favorite flower, which variety would they pick and when does it flower?

What is the favorite flower of Rose?

Gerberas.

What other daisy-like bloom is she fond of?

Japanese anemones.

Can you name two colors of her favorite flower that Hyacinth
particularly likes?

Yellow or orange.

What variety of rose would Rose pick?

Maiden's Blush.

What color of her namesake flower would Hyacinth choose?

Violet-blue.

For their joint favorite flower, which variety would they pick and
when does it flower?

Stromboli; in mid-summer.

See if you can work out how much time has elapsed between each of these pairs of times.

4:55a.m. to 6:15p.m. = [:   ]

8:10a.m. to 12:25p.m. = [:   ]

2:45a.m. to 7:10p.m. = [:   ]

12:20p.m. to 12:35p.m. = [:   ]

12:35a.m. to 1:15p.m. = [:   ]

3:05a.m. to 1:35p.m. = [:   ]

10:00a.m. to 11:25a.m. = [:   ]

9:50a.m. to 11:15p.m. = [:   ]

2:40a.m. to 1:30p.m. = [:   ]

12:00p.m. to 10:35p.m. = [:   ]

11:55a.m. to 9:55p.m. = [:   ]

1:50a.m. to 9:30a.m. = [:   ]

6:50p.m. to 8:45p.m. = [:   ]

8:05a.m. to 6:30p.m. = [:   ]

The solutions are:

4:55a.m.	to	6:15p.m. =	**13:20**
8:10a.m.	to	12:25p.m. =	**4:15**
2:45a.m.	to	7:10p.m. =	**16:25**
12:20p.m.	to	12:35p.m. =	**0:15**
12:35a.m.	to	1:15p.m. =	**12:40**
3:05a.m.	to	1:35p.m. =	**10:30**
10:00a.m.	to	11:25a.m. =	**1:25**
9:50a.m.	to	11:15p.m. =	**13:25**
2:40a.m.	to	1:30p.m. =	**10:50**
12:00p.m.	to	10:35p.m. =	**10:35**
11:55a.m.	to	9:55p.m. =	**10:00**
1:50a.m.	to	9:30a.m. =	**7:40**
6:50p.m.	to	8:45p.m. =	**1:55**
8:05a.m.	to	6:30p.m. =	**10:25**

Look at the following picture. In just one minute see if you can reproduce it precisely as if reflected in the vertical line "mirror." Draw the result on the empty grid to the right of the mirror line.

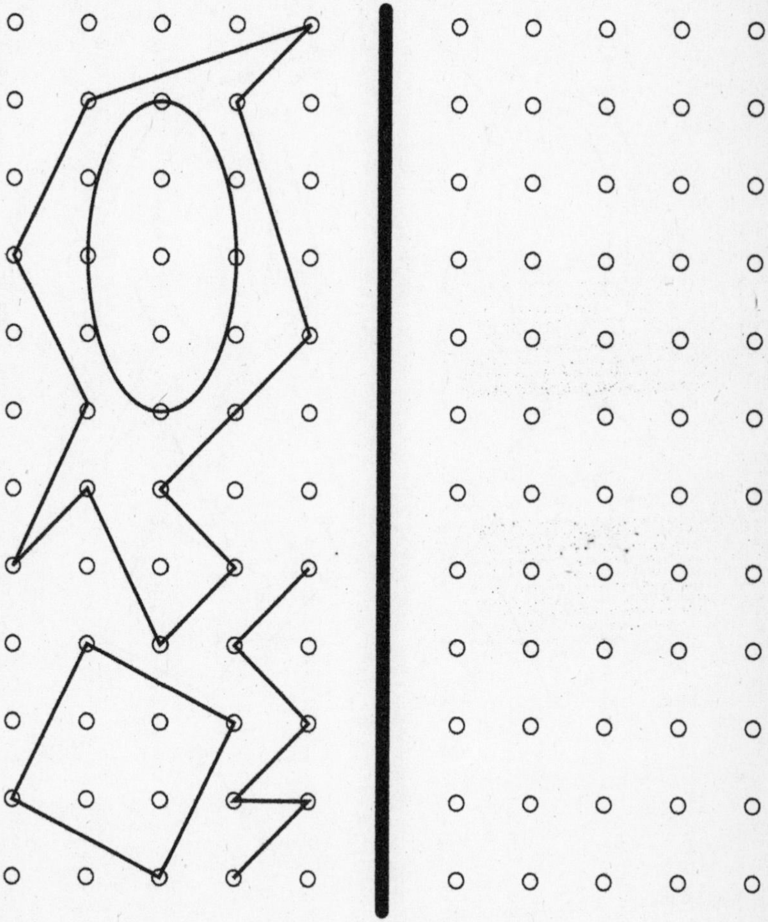

The reflected picture should look like this:

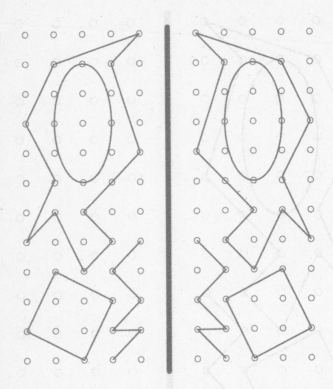

Look at this picture, then try to answer the following counting questions.

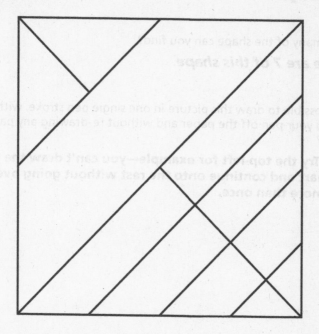

How many triangles can you find in this picture? ____

How many of the following shape can you find? ____

Is it possible to draw this picture in one single pen stroke, without taking your pen off the paper and without re-drawing any part of a line? ____

How many triangles can you find in this picture?

16 triangles.

How many of the shape can you find?

There are 7 of this shape.

Is it possible to draw this picture in one single pen stroke, without taking your pen off the paper and without re-drawing any part of a line?

No. **Try the top-left for example—you can't draw the top-left part and continue onto the rest without going over a line more than once.**

What is the longest path you can find in this number maze that moves from square to square by applying the operation "−17"? Squares must touch horizontally or vertically. Mark it in.

186	32	46	60	89
16	172	57	74	91
158	23	40	88	108
8	144	102	142	125
140	116	130	159	174

Now try to find a second path by applying "−14," but this time you may also move to diagonally touching squares. Mark in the longest path you can find.

The solutions are:

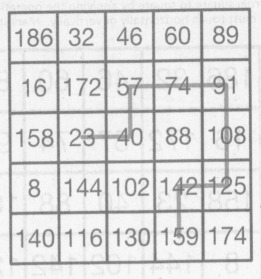

9 squares

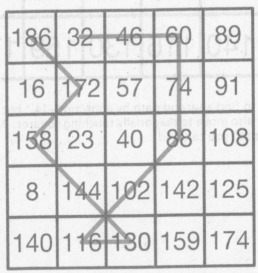

12 squares

Can you work out which of the shapes at the bottom of this page can be joined together to make the larger shape at the top? None of the pieces can be rotated or turned over, and no shape can be used more than once.

The solution and shapes are:

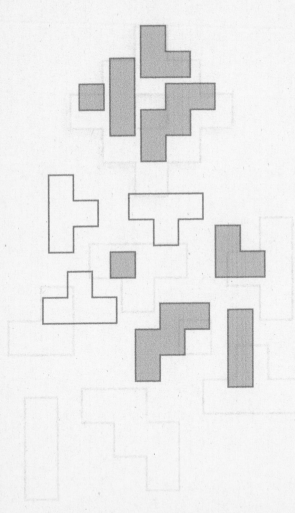

Look at the following list of computer peripherals for up to two minutes. On the following page you will find the same list of words but in a different order—turn the page and see how accurately you can recall the correct positioning of the words.

Keyboard	Mouse	Hard-drive	CD-drive
Processor	Memory	Webcam	Scanner
Tablet	Monitor	Network	Cable

MISSING WORDS 4

Once you have completed and checked the above task, try this one. Look at these two lists of words, then turn the page and try to spot which word is missing from each list.

Parrot	Jabiru	Crane
Pigeon	Gull	Goose

Radon	Oxygen	Hydrogen
Argon	Helium	Xenon

Try to place the words back in the appropriate boxes:

Cable	Memory	Processor
CD-drive	Monitor	Scanner
Hard-drive	Mouse	Tablet
Keyboard	Network	Webcam

MISSING WORDS 4

Can you spot which word is missing from each list?

Gull	Crane	Goose
Jabiru	Parrot	_____

Xenon	Helium	Radon
Hydrogen	Oxygen	_____

Can you draw three straight lines in order to divide this shape into four separate areas? The lines may touch but they must not cross, and they must not cross the shape outline. Each area must contain precisely one star, one circle and one hexagon.

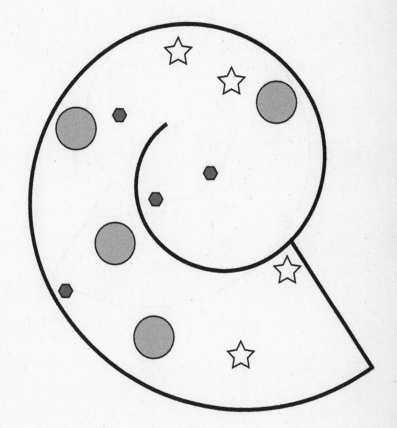

The solution is:

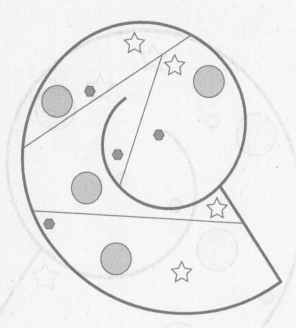

Try to complete the following arithmetic problems as quickly as possible:

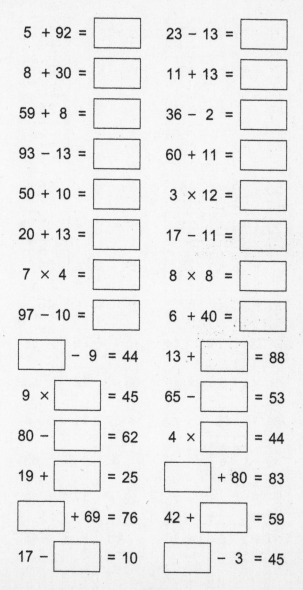

5 + 92 = ☐   23 − 13 = ☐

8 + 30 = ☐   11 + 13 = ☐

59 + 8 = ☐   36 − 2 = ☐

93 − 13 = ☐   60 + 11 = ☐

50 + 10 = ☐   3 × 12 = ☐

20 + 13 = ☐   17 − 11 = ☐

7 × 4 = ☐   8 × 8 = ☐

97 − 10 = ☐   6 + 40 = ☐

☐ − 9 = 44   13 + ☐ = 88

9 × ☐ = 45   65 − ☐ = 53

80 − ☐ = 62   4 × ☐ = 44

19 + ☐ = 25   ☐ + 80 = 83

☐ + 69 = 76   42 + ☐ = 59

17 − ☐ = 10   ☐ − 3 = 45

The solutions are:

5 + 92 = **97**	23 − 13 = **10**
8 + 30 = **38**	11 + 13 = **24**
59 + 8 = **67**	36 − 2 = **34**
93 − 13 = **80**	60 + 11 = **71**
50 + 10 = **60**	3 × 12 = **36**
20 + 13 = **33**	17 − 11 = **6**
7 × 4 = **28**	8 × 8 = **64**
97 − 10 = **87**	6 + 40 = **46**
53 − 9 = 44	13 + **75** = 88
9 × **5** = 45	65 − **12** = 53
80 − **18** = 62	4 × **11** = 44
19 + **6** = 25	**3** + 80 = 83
7 + 69 = 76	42 + **17** = 59
17 − **7** = 10	**48** − 3 = 45

Consider these numbers:

2   7   15   3

        21   4   12   9

Can you find *five* sets of two numbers which add together to make a third?

___ + ___ = ___

___ + ___ = ___

___ + ___ = ___

___ + ___ = ___

___ + ___ = ___

Now find two sets of two numbers which *multiply* together to make a third number.

___ × ___ = ___

___ × ___ = ___

Can you find five sets of two numbers which add together to make a third?

The five sets are:

$$4 + 3 = 7$$
$$2 + 7 = 9$$
$$3 + 9 = 12$$
$$3 + 12 = 15$$
$$9 + 12 = 21$$

Now find two sets of two numbers which multiply together to make a third number.

The two sets are:

$$4 \times 3 = 12$$
$$3 \times 7 = 21$$

Look at the following picture for up to two minutes, then rotate the book *clockwise* and cover over the top half of the page. Now try to reproduce the picture on the empty grid.

Now rotate the book back, uncover the top half again and check for and correct any mistakes.

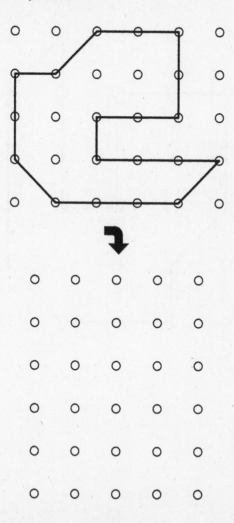

The rotated version of the picture should look like this:

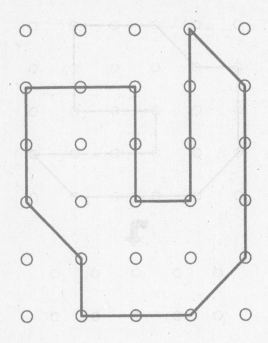

If you were to cut out this shape net consisting of four adjacent triangles and fold it up into a pyramid, which of the four pictures below would be visible by rotating the pyramid appropriately?

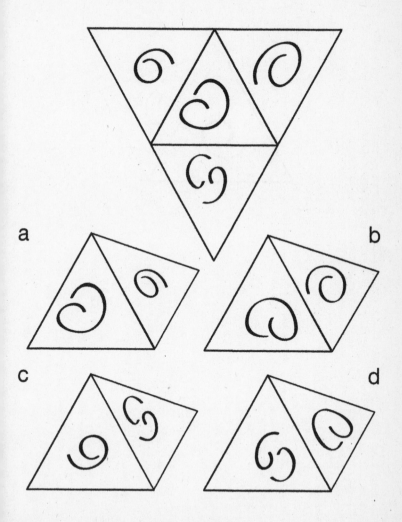

a

b

c

d

The only arrangement that would be visible is:

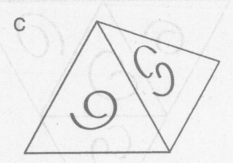

Can you place the numbers 1 to 9 into each of the empty boxes so that no number is used more than once and so that each of the arithmetic equations reading both across and down is correct?

You don't need to guess—only logic is required!

Work out values as if typing the sums into a calculator—so for example in the first column multiply the first two numbers before multiplying by the third.

The solution is:

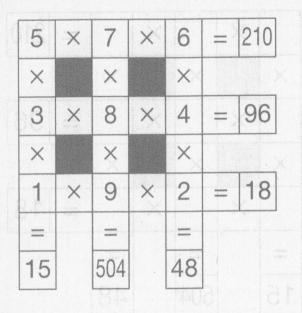

5	×	7	×	6	=	210
×		×		×		
3	×	8	×	4	=	96
×		×		×		
1	×	9	×	2	=	18
=		=		=		
15		504		48		

Which of these vegetables is the odd one out, and why?

Carrot	Potato	Swede
Parsnip	Sprout	Turnip

Which number comes next in this sequence?

1   3   3   9   27   _____

If I have two £5 notes and two £10 notes in my pocket, what is the likelihood that I randomly pull out two notes that add up to £15? _____

I run twelve times around a 400-meter circuit, and then walk another 200 meters. If this all takes me an hour, what has my average speed been?

48 strawberry and 36 blackcurrant jelly beans are in a jar. If I eat half of the beans of each flavor and then give a third of the remaining strawberry ones to a friend, how many are left in the jar?

If I add up the first 15 numbers, 1 to 15, what is the result? _____

Look at the following list of cakes and spend up to one minute trying to memorize all eight words. Then turn the page and recall as many as possible.

Carrot	Almond	Sponge	Fudge
Brownie	Cup	Angel	Pound

Which of these vegetables is the odd one out, and why?

Sprout—the rest are root vegetables.

Which number comes next in this sequence?

243—each number is multiplied by the preceding one.

If I have two £5 notes and two £10 notes in my pocket, what is the likelihood that I randomly pull out two notes that add up to £15?

2 in 3. I need one £5 note (2 in 4 chance) and one £10 note (2 in 3 chance), OR one £10 note (2 in 4 chance) and one £5 note (2 in 3 chance), so 2 times 2 in 4 times 2 in 3—this is 8 in 12, or 2 in 3.

I run twelve times around a 400-meter circuit, and then walk another 200 meters. If this all takes me an hour, what has my average speed been?

5 kilometers per hour, or 5,000 meters per hour.

48 strawberry and 36 blackcurrant jelly beans are in a jar. If I eat half of the beans of each flavor and then give a third of the remaining strawberry ones to a friend, how many are left in the jar?

34 beans. After eating I have 24+18 beans. I then give 8 of the 24 strawberry away, leaving 34.

If I add up the first 15 numbers, 1 to 15, what is the result?

120.

Recall the cakes:

*Read the following fantastical story, and then answer as many questions as you can **without** referring back to the text. Once you have answered as many as you can, read the text straight through one more time and see if you can then answer the rest.*

Tiptoeing across the landing, the quingle quaked. It was a strange and timid beast, and an unexpected sound quickened its already rapid heartbeat. The quiet was gone. Creaking things creaked and chattering things began to chatter. The lesser-spotted quingle was afraid.

In the dark, it heard a sleeping creature stir. Forgetting all attempt at stealth, the quingle ran. Feet flapping, it fled the fifth floor and almost fell down the flight of stairs. Crashing through an emergency exit, it flew with all the pace it could muster in its tired arms. "Away, away," the quaking quingle quacked to itself.

What two words beginning with "c" are used to describe why the quingle was first afraid?

What did the quingle hear stir in the dark?

Name two letters which are used alliteratively.

What did the quingle crash through?

What did the quingle say to itself at the end?

What floor had the quingle been on?

In what manner did the quingle walk across the landing initially?

What two words beginning with "c" are used to describe why the quingle was first afraid?

Creaking; chattering.

What did the quingle hear stir in the dark?

A sleeping creature.

Name two letters which are used alliteratively.

"q" and "f," and arguably "c" too.

What did the quingle crash through?

The emergency exit.

What did the quingle say to itself at the end?

"Away, away."

What floor had the quingle been on?

The fifth floor.

In what manner did the quingle walk across the landing initially?

Tiptoeing.

Look at this picture, then try to answer the following counting questions.

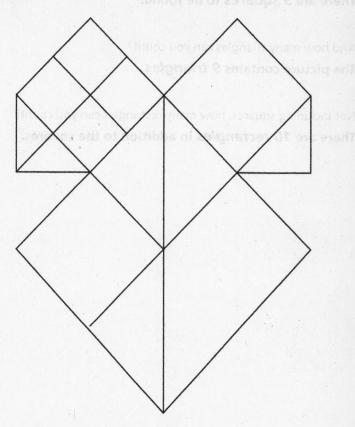

How many squares can you find in this picture? ____

And how many triangles can you count? ____

Not including squares, how many rectangles can you count? ____

How many squares can you find in this picture?
There are *9 squares* to be found.

And how many triangles can you count?
The picture contains *9 triangles*.

Not including squares, how many rectangles can you count?
There are *10 rectangles* in addition to the squares.

Fill in the empty bricks in this *multiplication* number pyramid. Each brick must contain a number equal to the *product* of the two bricks directly below it.

Only whole numbers may be used.

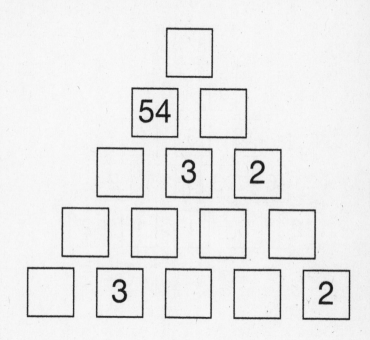

The solution is:

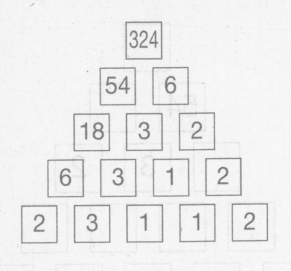

Try to complete the following arithmetic problems as quickly as possible:

6 × 9 = ☐   10 + 86 = ☐

13 + 18 = ☐   15 + 34 = ☐

20 + 61 = ☐   3 + 17 = ☐

8 × 12 = ☐   89 + 8 = ☐

76 + 6 = ☐   86 − 16 = ☐

94 − 6 = ☐   58 − 17 = ☐

39 − 17 = ☐   11 + 9 = ☐

54 − 17 = ☐   50 − 20 = ☐

39 − ☐ = 24   25 − ☐ = 11

☐ + 83 = 93   ☐ × 6 = 60

24 − ☐ = 5   12 × ☐ = 108

☐ − 9 = 47   77 − ☐ = 74

8 × ☐ = 48   ☐ − 15 = 38

103 − ☐ = 83   9 + ☐ = 70

The solutions are:

$6 \times 9 =$ **54** $\qquad$ $10 + 86 =$ **96**

$13 + 18 =$ **31** $\qquad$ $15 + 34 =$ **49**

$20 + 61 =$ **81** $\qquad$ $3 + 17 =$ **20**

$8 \times 12 =$ **96** $\qquad$ $89 + 8 =$ **97**

$76 + 6 =$ **82** $\qquad$ $86 - 16 =$ **70**

$94 - 6 =$ **88** $\qquad$ $58 - 17 =$ **41**

$39 - 17 =$ **22** $\qquad$ $11 + 9 =$ **20**

$54 - 17 =$ **37** $\qquad$ $50 - 20 =$ **30**

$39 -$ **15** $= 24$ $\qquad$ $25 -$ **14** $= 11$

10 $+ 83 = 93$ $\qquad$ **10** $\times 6 = 60$

$24 -$ **19** $= 5$ $\qquad$ $12 \times$ **9** $= 108$

56 $- 9 = 47$ $\qquad$ $77 -$ **3** $= 74$

$8 \times$ **6** $= 48$ $\qquad$ **53** $- 15 = 38$

$103 -$ **20** $= 83$ $\qquad$ $9 +$ **61** $= 70$

Which of these is the odd one out, and why?

| Widow | Silk | Curtain |
| Orb | Jumping | Hunting |

Which number comes next in this sequence?

| 1 | 2 | 6 | 24 | 120 | ___ |

If each minute of an hour lost 10 seconds, how many minutes long would an hour be in order to preserve the normal number of seconds?

If I roll a six-sided dice twice, what is the likelihood that I roll a total of 4?

___

If a dog has seven puppies, and each of its six female puppies has seven more puppies, how many dogs is that that I have mentioned in total?

___

To convert Fahrenheit to Celsius you subtract 32, multiply by 5 and divide by 9. So it if is 95 degrees Fahrenheit, what is the temperature in Celsius?

___

Look at the following list and spend up to one minute trying to memorize all nine words. Then turn the page and recall as many as possible.

Diary	Album	Comic
Annual	Manual	Novella
Scrapbook	Dictionary	Jotter

Which of these is the odd one out, and why?

***Curtain*—all the rest are types of spider.**

Which number comes next in this sequence?

***720.* Each is the previous number multiplied by 2, 3, 4 etc.—in other words, the factorial numbers.**

If each minute of an hour lost 10 seconds, how many minutes long would an hour be in order to preserve the same number of seconds?

***72 minutes.* 60 lots of 10 seconds = 600 seconds would be lost, so we'd need an additional 600/50 minutes = 12 extra minutes.**

If I roll a six-sided dice twice, what is the likelihood that I roll a total of 4?

***3 in 36,* since there are 6x6 = 36 possibilities, and either 1-3, 3-1 or 2-2 out of these will equal 4.**

If a dog has seven puppies, and each of its six female puppies has seven more puppies, how many dogs is that that I have mentioned in total?

***50 dogs.* 1 dog + 7 puppies + (6x7 = 42).**

To convert Fahrenheit to Celsius you subtract 32, multiply by 5 and divide by 9. So it if is 95 degrees Fahrenheit, what is the temperature in Celsius?

35 degrees Celsius.

Recall the words:

Look at the following picture. In just one minute see if you can reproduce it precisely as if reflected in the diagonal line "mirror." Draw the result on the empty grid below the mirror line.

Rotating the book might make it easier, but avoid doing so if you can help it!

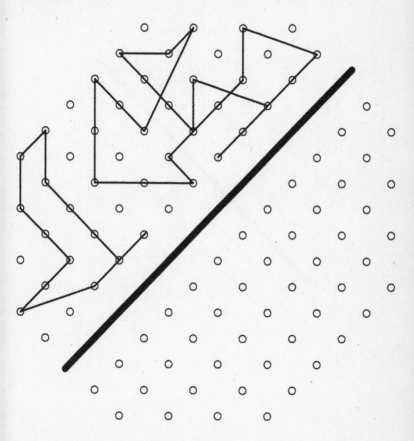

The reflected picture should look like this:

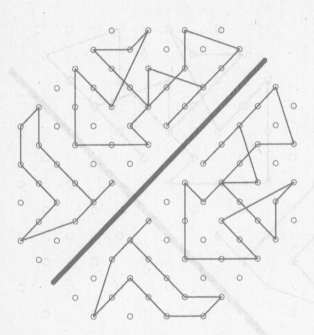

Look at the following list of European languages for up to two minutes. On the following page you will find the same list of words but in a different order—turn the page and see how accurately you can recall the correct positioning of the words.

Hungarian	Icelandic	Sardinian
Slovene	Italian	Danish
Polish	Zyrian	Ukrainian
Serbo-Croatian	Swedish	Spanish
Frisian	Catalan	Cornish

Bonus marks if you can place where all of these are spoken on a map!

MISSING WORDS 5

Once you have completed and checked the above task, try this one. Look at these two lists of words, then turn the page and try to spot which word is missing from each list.

Pythagoras	Newton	Pascal	Turing
	Einstein	Lagrange	Euclid

Endless	Ages	Eon	Yore
	Past	Bygone	Epochal

Try to place the words back in the appropriate boxes:

Catalan	Icelandic	Slovene
Cornish	Italian	Spanish
Danish	Polish	Swedish
Frisian	Sardinian	Ukrainian
Hungarian	Serbo-Croatian	Zyrian

MISSING WORDS 5

Can you spot which word is missing from each list?

Euclid	Lagrange	Pascal	_____
Newton	Pythagoras	Einstein	

Eon	Past	Bygone	_____
Epochal	Yore	Endless	

Can you place the numbers 1 to 9 into each of the empty boxes so that no number is used more than once and so that each of the arithmetic equations reading both across and down is correct?

You don't need to guess—only logic is required!

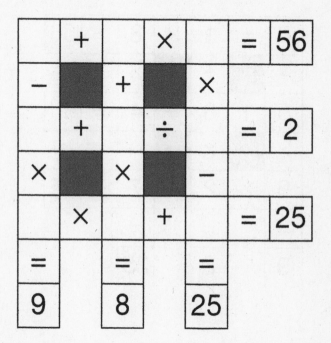

Work out values as if typing the sums into a calculator—so for example in the first row add the first two numbers before multiplying by the third.

The solution is:

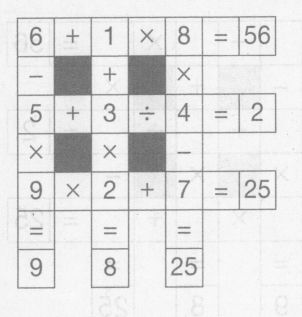

6	+	1	×	8	=	56
−		+		×		
5	+	3	÷	4	=	2
×		×		−		
9	×	2	+	7	=	25
=		=		=		
9		8		25		

See if you can work out how much time has elapsed between each of these pairs of times.

8:10p.m. to 11:05p.m. = [:]

2:05a.m. to 11:15a.m. = [:]

2:25p.m. to 7:30p.m. = [:]

5:40a.m. to 1:25p.m. = [:]

12:05a.m. to 6:30p.m. = [:]

7:20p.m. to 9:05p.m. = [:]

8:15p.m. to 10:45p.m. = [:]

4:35a.m. to 6:55a.m. = [:]

8:10a.m. to 12:50p.m. = [:]

7:35a.m. to 11:45a.m. = [:]

2:50a.m. to 1:55p.m. = [:]

3:10a.m. to 7:35a.m. = [:]

1:45a.m. to 4:30p.m. = [:]

11:45a.m. to 1:35p.m. = [:]

The solutions are:

8:10p.m.	to	11:05p.m. =	**2:55**
2:05a.m.	to	11:15a.m. =	**9:10**
2:25p.m.	to	7:30p.m. =	**5:05**
5:40a.m.	to	1:25p.m. =	**7:45**
12:05a.m.	to	6:30p.m. =	**18:25**
7:20p.m.	to	9:05p.m. =	**1:45**
8:15p.m.	to	10:45p.m. =	**2:30**
4:35a.m.	to	6:55a.m. =	**2:20**
8:10a.m.	to	12:50p.m. =	**4:40**
7:35a.m.	to	11:45a.m. =	**4:10**
2:50a.m.	to	1:55p.m. =	**11:05**
3:10a.m.	to	7:35a.m. =	**4:25**
1:45a.m.	to	4:30p.m. =	**14:45**
11:45a.m.	to	1:35p.m. =	**1:50**

Can you draw **two squares** in order to divide this existing square shape into four separate areas? Each area must contain precisely one star, one circle and one hexagon.

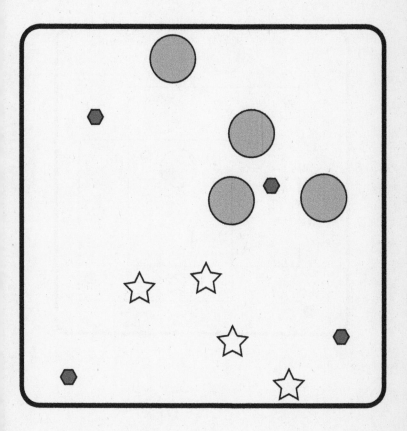

The solution is:

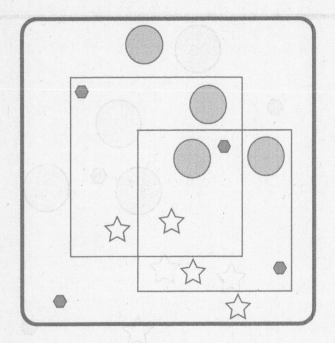

What is the longest path you can find in this number maze that moves from square to square by either one of the two operations "+9" and "+15"? Squares must touch horizontally or vertically. Use both operations in the path, but only one per move.

79	93	102	111	137
84	64	59	68	124
75	35	44	77	92
26	62	53	116	101
71	17	140	125	136

Now try to find a second path by using "+9" and "+13," but this time you may also move to diagonally touching squares. Mark in the longest path you can find.

The solutions are:

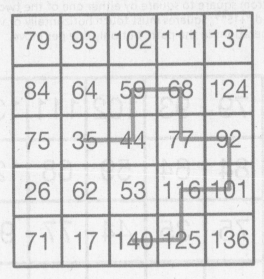

10 squares

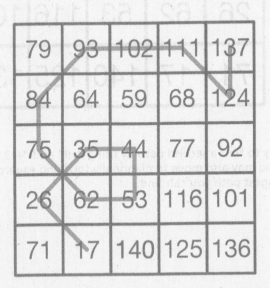

13 squares

If you were to cut out this shape net consisting of six adjacent squares and fold it up into a cube, which of the three shapes below would be visible by rotating the cube appropriately?

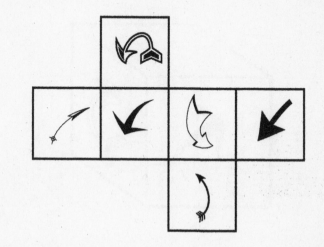

a

b

c

The only arrangement that would be visible is:

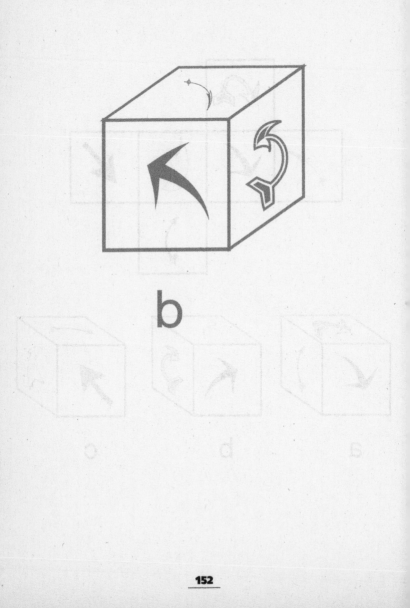

b

Look at the following picture for up to two minutes, then rotate the book upside down and cover over the top half of the page. Now try to reproduce the picture on the empty grid.

Now rotate the book back, uncover the top half again and check for and correct any mistakes.

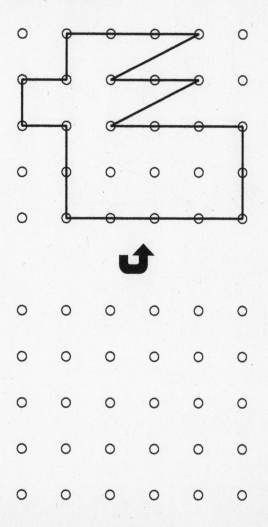

The rotated version of the picture should look like this:

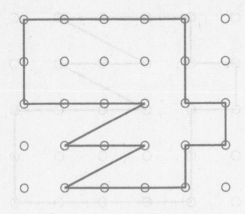

Consider these numbers:

17   36   15   19

     23   14   37

Can you find two numbers which add together to make a third?

____ + ____ = ____

Now find a different set of two numbers which add together to make a third number.

____ + ____ = ____

Can you find three numbers that add together to give a total of 87?

____ + ____ + ____ = 87

How many of these are prime numbers (only divisible by themselves and one)?   ____

Can you find two numbers which add together to make a third? And a different set?

The two sets are:

$$23 + 14 = 37$$
$$17 + 19 = 36$$

Can you find three numbers that add together to give a total of 87?

$$14 + 36 + 37 = 87$$

How many of these are prime numbers (only divisible by themselves and one)?

4 prime numbers. **They are 17, 19, 23 and 37.**

Can you work out which of the shapes at the bottom of this page can be joined together to make the larger shape at the top? None of the pieces can be rotated or turned over, and no shape can be used more than once.

The solution and shapes are:

Fill in the empty bricks in this number pyramid. Each brick must contain a number equal to the sum of the *three* bricks closest to it on the line below.

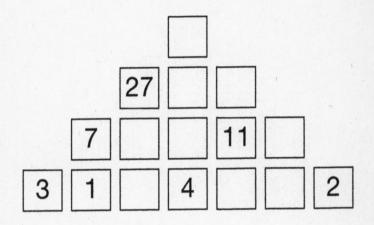

The solution is:

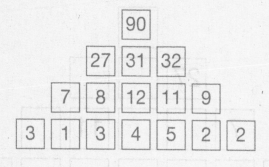

Can you draw **two circles** in order to divide this square shape into four separate areas? Each area must contain precisely one star, one of the existing shaded circles and one hexagon.

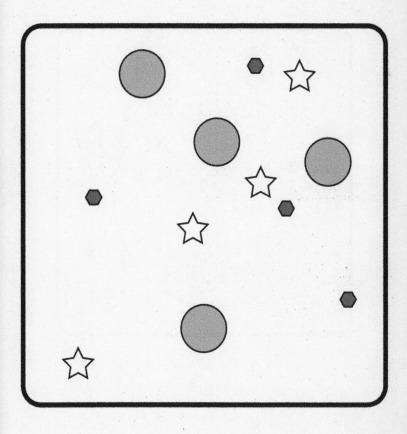

The solution is:

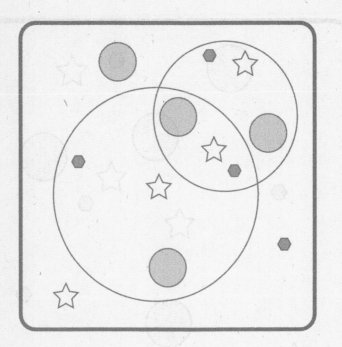

Try to complete the following arithmetic problems as quickly as possible:

7 + 23 = ☐   103 − 3 = ☐

73 + 13 = ☐   9 × 4 = ☐

90 + 20 = ☐   17 + 4 = ☐

71 − 3 = ☐   3 + 90 = ☐

86 + 15 = ☐   34 + 5 = ☐

98 + 19 = ☐   82 + 10 = ☐

63 − 17 = ☐   95 + 18 = ☐

7 × 6 = ☐   10 × 6 = ☐

☐ + 15 = 72   ☐ × 4 = 16

14 + ☐ = 96   19 + ☐ = 32

84 − ☐ = 76   ☐ − 11 = 87

☐ − 3 = 5   13 + ☐ = 69

77 − ☐ = 70   ☐ − 10 = 54

50 − ☐ = 42   ☐ − 10 = 39

The solutions are:

7 + 23 = **30**   103 − 3 = **100**

73 + 13 = **86**   9 × 4 = **36**

90 + 20 = **110**   17 + 4 = **21**

71 − 3 = **68**   3 + 90 = **93**

86 + 15 = **101**   34 + 5 = **39**

98 + 19 = **117**   82 + 10 = **92**

63 − 17 = **46**   95 + 18 = **113**

7 × 6 = **42**   10 × 6 = **60**

57 + 15 = 72   **4** × 4 = 16

14 + **82** = 96   19 + **13** = 32

84 − **8** = 76   **98** − 11 = 87

8 − 3 = 5   13 + **56** = 69

77 − **7** = 70   **64** − 10 = 54

50 − **8** = 42   **49** − 10 = 39

Look at the following picture. In just a couple of minutes see if you can reproduce it precisely as if reflected in the diagonal line "mirror." Draw the result on the empty grid below the mirror line.

Rotating the book might make it easier, but avoid doing so if you can help it!

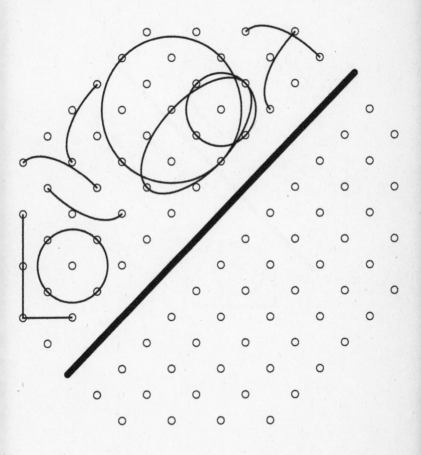

The reflected picture should look like this:

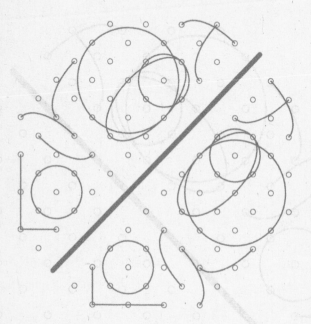

Look at the following list of film directors for up to two minutes. On the following page you will find the same list of words but in a different order—turn the page and see how accurately you can recall the correct positioning of the words.

Altman	De Palma	Ivory
Soderbergh	Scorsese	Spielberg
Attenborough	Romero	Scott
Leigh	Lucas	Loach
Zemeckis	Hitchcock	Kubrick

Bonus marks if you can also name a film by each of them!

MISSING WORDS 6

Once you have completed and checked the above task, try this one. Look at these two lists of words, then turn the page and try to spot which word is missing from each list.

Andrew   Peter   James   Matthew
     Thomas   Philip   Bartholomew

Bumper   Clutch   Gearbox   Fan
     Seat   Piston   Odometer

Try to place the words back in the appropriate boxes:

<table>
<tr><td></td><td></td><td></td></tr>
<tr><td></td><td></td><td></td></tr>
<tr><td></td><td></td><td></td></tr>
<tr><td></td><td></td><td></td></tr>
<tr><td></td><td></td><td></td></tr>
</table>

Altman	Kubrick	Scorsese
Attenborough	Leigh	Scott
De Palma	Loach	Soderbergh
Hitchcock	Lucas	Spielberg
Ivory	Romero	Zemeckis

MISSING WORDS 6

Can you spot which word is missing from each list?

Bartholomew **Thomas** **James** **Matthew**
Andrew **Peter** _____

Gearbox **Odometer** **Piston** _____
Clutch **Fan** **Bumper**

Can you place the numbers 1 to 9 into each of the empty boxes so that no number is used more than once and so that each of the arithmetic equations reading both across and down is correct?

You don't need to guess—only logic is required!

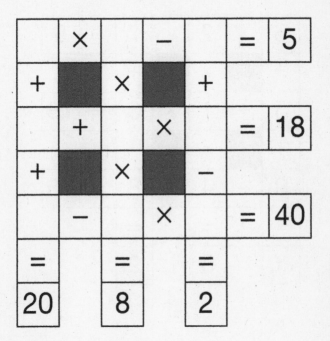

Work out values as if typing the sums into a calculator—so for example in the middle row add the first two numbers before multiplying by the third.

The solution is:

6	×	2	−	7	=	5
+		×		+		
5	+	1	×	3	=	18
+		×		−		
9	−	4	×	8	=	40
=		=		=		
20		8		2		

If you were to cut out this shape net consisting of six adjacent squares and fold it up into a cube, which of the three pictures below would be visible by rotating the cube appropriately?

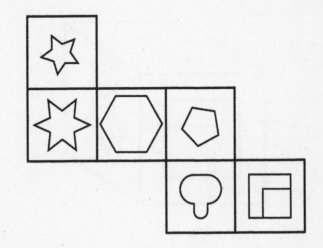

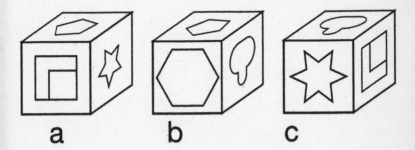

a   b   c

The only arrangement that would be visible is:

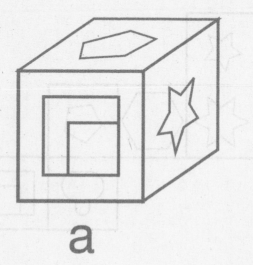

a

Look at this picture, then try to answer the following counting questions.

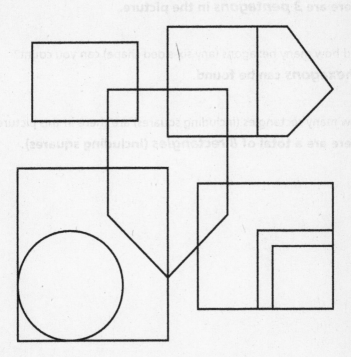

How many pentagons (any five-sided shape) can you count in this picture? ____

And how many hexagons (any six-sided shape) can you count? ____

How many rectangles (including squares) are there in this picture? ____

How many pentagons (any five-sided shape) can you count in this picture?

There are *3 pentagons* in the picture.

And how many hexagons (any six-sided shape) can you count?

***8 hexagons* can be found.**

How many rectangles (including squares) are there in this picture?

There are a total of *8 rectangles* (including squares).

What is the longest path you can find in this number maze that moves from square to square by applying one per move of the following operations? Squares must touch horizontally or vertically.

×3   ÷4   +5   −6

51	56	14	8	24
17	10	40	35	18
12	4	135	140	54
74	51	45	12	48
68	17	18	6	24

Now try to find a second path by applying the following operations. This time you may also move to diagonally touching squares.

×2   ÷3   −4   +6

The solutions are:

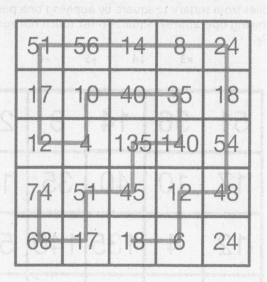

51 56 14 8 24
17 10 40 35 18
12 4 135 140 54
74 51 45 12 48
68 17 18 6 24

24 squares

51 56 14 8 24
17 10 40 35 18
12 4 135 140 54
74 51 45 12 48
68 17 18 6 24

11 squares

Look at the following picture for up to two minutes, then do not rotate the book but simply cover the top half of the page. Now try to reproduce the picture on the empty grid, rotated through 180 degrees.

Now uncover the top half again and check for and correct any mistakes.

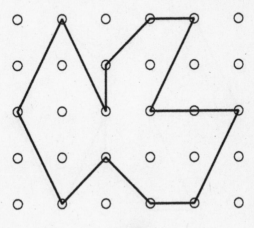

The rotated version of the picture should look like this:

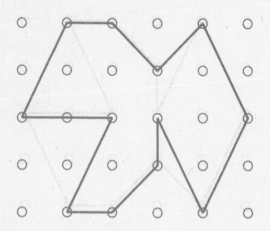

Can you work out which of the shapes at the bottom of this page can be joined together to make the larger shape at the top? None of the pieces can be rotated or turned over, and no shape can be used more than once.

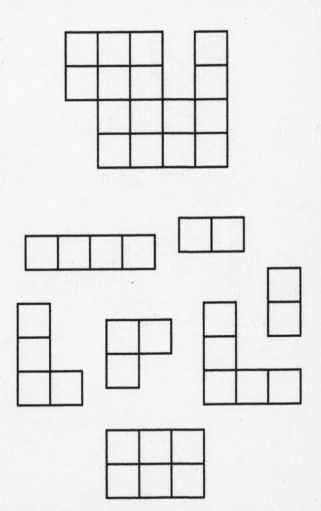

The solution and shapes are:

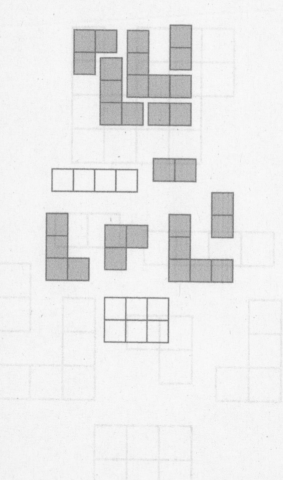

See if you can work out how much time has elapsed between each of these pairs of times.

2:05a.m. to 6:25a.m. = [:]

9:10a.m. to 11:00p.m. = [:]

5:05a.m. to 8:40a.m. = [:]

11:30a.m. to 11:35a.m. = [:]

12:30a.m. to 9:45p.m. = [:]

6:45p.m. to 10:10p.m. = [:]

8:20a.m. to 10:50p.m. = [:]

3:35p.m. to 5:05p.m. = [:]

12:50a.m. to 1:00p.m. = [:]

11:40a.m. to 9:50p.m. = [:]

4:05a.m. to 2:35p.m. = [:]

12:10a.m. to 7:20p.m. = [:]

1:25p.m. to 8:05p.m. = [:]

5:05a.m. to 8:35p.m. = [:]

The solutions are:

2:05a.m.	to 6:25a.m. =	**4:20**
9:10a.m.	to 11:00p.m. =	**13:50**
5:05a.m.	to 8:40a.m. =	**3:35**
11:30a.m.	to 11:35a.m. =	**0:05**
12:30a.m.	to 9:45p.m. =	**21:15**
6:45p.m.	to 10:10p.m. =	**3:25**
8:20a.m.	to 10:50p.m. =	**14:30**
3:35p.m.	to 5:05p.m. =	**1:30**
12:50a.m.	to 1:00p.m. =	**12:10**
11:40a.m.	to 9:50p.m. =	**10:10**
4:05a.m.	to 2:35p.m. =	**10:30**
12:10a.m.	to 7:20p.m. =	**19:10**
1:25p.m.	to 8:05p.m. =	**6:40**
5:05a.m.	to 8:35p.m. =	**15:30**

Which of these is the odd one out, and why?

Paper	Ruby	Gold
Plastic	Silver	Cotton

Which number comes next in this sequence?

1   4   6   8   9   10   ____

And which letter comes next in this sequence?

B   C   D   G   J   ____

If I toss a coin four times, what is the likelihood I
get four tails?   ____

I sell 85% of my 2,000 shares, making 20% profit on each
share. I originally paid £6,000 for all 2,000. Assuming no
fees are paid, how much profit did I just receive?   ____

If a perfectly flat and square table has an area of 16 meters
squared, how long is each side?   ____

What is the product of all the numbers from 1 to 8
inclusive?   ____

Look at the following list of words and spend up to one minute
trying to memorize all nine words. Then turn the page and recall
as many as possible.

Asset	Lease	Tariff
Capital	Budget	Subsidy
Payroll	Interest	Trade

Which of these is the odd one out, and why?

***Plastic*—the rest are traditional wedding anniversaries.**

Which number comes next in this sequence?

12—it is a list of the non-prime numbers.

And which letter comes next in this sequence?

O—the next letter that is curved when upper-case.

If I toss a coin four times, what is the likelihood I get four tails?

1 in 16, which is 1 in 2 multiplied by itself 4 times.

I sell 85% of my 2,000 shares, making 20% profit on each share. I originally paid £6,000 for all 2,000. Assuming no fees are paid, how much profit did I just receive?

£1,020. I originally paid £6,000 for 2,000 shares, or £3/ share. I now make 20% profit, so £0.60/share. I sell 1,700 shares (85% of 2,000).

If a perfectly flat and square table has an area of 16 meters squared, how long is each side?

4 meters on each side, since 4 times 4 is 16.

What is the product of all the numbers from 1 to 8 inclusive?

40320.

Recall the financial terms:

*Read the following poetic revelation, and then answer as many
questions as you can **without** referring back to the text. Once you
have answered as many as you can, read the text straight through
one more time and see if you can then answer the rest.*

In the last defeat of a glorious winter,
My smiling year of torment fell,
Down the stream of bitter memory,
Washed away on a tidal swell.

Broken pieces outward flew,
My re-enchantment wrought the air,
Rent right through with chastened haste,
From lost in time to self-aware.

In true alliance with my soul,
I fought until I found my face,
Toiled upward to my grail,
And found at end a settled grace.

What was it the "smiling year" of?
What was I allied with?
What "wrought the air"?
What is described as flying outward?
What is finally defeated?
What I had previously been lost to?
What did I fight until I found?
What was it that I toiled upward to?

What was it the "smiling year" of?
Torment.

What was I allied with?
My soul.

What "wrought the air"?
My re-enchantment.

What is described as flying outward?
Broken pieces.

What is finally defeated?
A glorious winter.

What I had previously been lost to?
Time.

What did I fight until I found?
My face.

What was it that I toiled upward to?
My grail.

Consider these numbers:

18	9	38	16
31	24	7	40

Can you find **four** sets of two numbers which add together to make a third?

___ + ___ = ___

___ + ___ = ___

___ + ___ = ___

___ + ___ = ___

What is the highest whole multiple of 4 that you can achieve by adding any two numbers together?   ___

How many of these are prime numbers (only divisible by themselves and one)?

What is the sum of the five smallest numbers?   ___

Can you find four sets of two numbers which add together to make a third?

The four sets are:

$$7 + 24 = 31$$
$$31 + 9 = 40$$
$$16 + 24 = 40$$
$$9 + 7 = 16$$

What is the highest whole multiple of 4 that you can achieve by adding any two numbers together?

64, which is 16×4, formed by 24+40.

How many of these are prime numbers (only divisible by themselves and one)?

2 prime numbers, which are 7 and 31.

What is the sum of the 5 smallest numbers?

74. 7+9+16+18+24.

If the regular Cardiff to Reading train leaves Cardiff at 3:50p.m. and travels at an average speed of 60m.p.h., but the Cardiff to Reading express train leaves at 4:15p.m. and travels at 80m.p.h., which will arrive first? Both trains travel along 100 miles of track.

If Whining Whinny has 3:1 odds of winning the Grand Chase horse race, Wandering Wonzo has 2:1 odds on the Large Leaps steeplechase, and Wild Wallion has 3:2 odds on the Galloping Ground race—and if these odds reflect their true statistical likelihood of winning the race—then what is the chance of all three horses winning their respective races?

My apple orchard has eighteen apple trees in it, and each tree has 100 apples on it. This spring, however, a third of the trees died, and of the remainder, 40% of the fruit was lost to birds. If I can put six apples in a bag, how many bags of apples can I produce from this year's remaining fruit?

Which number comes next in this sequence?

5   6   4   7   3   8   ____

If you replace numbers with letters so that A=1, B=2, C=3 etc., what is the result of the following sums?

ABC + GHI = ____   **ADF – EE = ____**

If you had spent exactly two minutes on each Beginners' page of puzzles in this book, three minutes on each Intermediate page and four minutes on each Advanced page, how long would it have taken you in total to complete this book? ____

Try this riddle: what is lighter than a feather and has nothing in it, but even the strongest person cannot hold it for more than a few minutes? _____

Which train will arrive first?

Both arrive at the same time. **The first train takes 1 hour 40 and the second takes 1 hour 15, so both arrive at 5:30p.m.**

What is the chance of all three horses winning their respective races?

9:1, **or 1/9, which is 1 in 3 times 1 in 2 times 2 in 3, or in other words 2 in 18.**

How many bags of apples can I produce from this year's remaining fruit?

120 bags. **You lose six trees and then have sixty apples left on each remaining tree.**

Which number comes next in the sequence?

2. **The sequence is formed by applying +1, –2, +3, –4, +5 etc.**

If you replace numbers with letters so that A=1, B=2, C=3 etc., what is the result of the following sums?

ABC + GHI = IAB   ***ADF – EE = IA***

since

123 + 789 = 912   **146 – 55 = 91**

How long would it have taken you in total to complete this book?

274 minutes. **There are 30, 30 and 31 puzzle pages in each section respectively, so that's 30x2 + 30x3 + 31x4.**

What is lighter than a feather and has nothing in it, but even the strongest person cannot hold it for more than a few minutes?

Your breath.